On Sunday March 21

word from God ever. He has been walking me slowly through my destiny. I know that a lot of Church of Christ members are going to be upset but I know that more than enough are going to say "Thank You". There are so many of us that have been suppressing these awesome gifts from God and it is time to stop so that our Churches grow as God wants them to. We speak about these things among certain people because we don't want everyone else to know and be outed in church by the pastors and the members. It is now time to stand up because we have done nothing wrong and God is for us. Am I saying that we are special? I am saying that God gave the gifts to us because we are able to handle the walk that comes with the gift. It is time to stop concealing and start learning and grow with the gift. Let us grow.

1 Corinthians 12

1Now concerning spiritual gifts, brethren, I would not have you ignorant. 2Ye know that ye were Gentiles, carried away unto these dumb idols, even as ye were led. 3Wherefore I give you to understand, that no man speaking by the Spirit of God calleth Jesus accursed: and that no man can say that Jesus is the Lord, but by the Holy Ghost. 4Now there are diversities of gifts, but the same Spirit. 5And there are differences of administrations, but the same Lord. 6And there are diversities of operations, but it is the same God which worketh all in all. 7But the manifestation of the Spirit is given to every man to profit withal. 8For to one is given by the Spirit the word of wisdom; to another the word of knowledge by the same Spirit; 9To another faith by the same Spirit; to another the gifts of healing by the same Spirit; 10To another the working of miracles; to another prophecy; to another discerning of spirits; to another divers kinds of tongues; to another the interpretation of tongues: 11But all these worketh that one and the selfsame Spirit, dividing to every man severally as he will.

4

Contents

Chapter 1

Spiritual Gifts

We are going to take a moment to go over the gifts that were spoken and given to us by God. Christ was able to perform all these miracles. He showed and illustrated to those in the early church how to use these great gifts to help fight the enemy. These gifts were not laid down with Him when He died and rose again. Notice He rose again when He rose the gifts were alive. We are to learn how to use these gifts as they are given to us. When we are given these gifts the Book is the instruction manual on how to use the gifts and so many of us are made aware of them but because we don't want to go through the warfare we try to suppress them. There is nothing new under the sun. We are not performing anything that has not already been done before. If you read the word the gifts were not just utilized to generate the faith of those but it was also a combat tactic to assist in the fight of the enemy. We are not done fighting the enemy he is still here fighting us on a daily basis. With these gifts some are able to make the demon possession of some go away. Some are able to see things before they happen or even some things that have already occurred in our paths. I know for many of us this book is going to give you the strength to fight those that don't want to believe. I apologize that it took me so long to hold onto the unchanging hand of God and deliver this message that has been on my heart for so many years. Now let us get down to the brass tactics of the Spiritual Gifts. Not all of us are able to have acquired spiritual gifts because we ask not maybe or because we may not know what to do with them. I don't know. I only can truly speak to those of us who are experiencing the great gifts from God. When we look at 1 Corinthians 12 we read about the diversities of gifts. We are told that there are diversities of gifts, but the same Spirit. This is telling us that there are many gifts because the definition for diverse is differing from one another : composed of distinct or unlike elements or qualities. We know that as we fight the enemy we have to know that he is not going to come after you the same way every time. He is going to try to use other things to get you off of your path. The path that you are traveling down you are knocked off the same way then he knows that it works so he is not going to try something new so he will continue to use the same tactics on you to get you to stop trying to serve God. The devil doesn't want you to talk to Jesus concerning anything. He doesn't want you to do anything but end up in hell with him. You will fall into this trap sometimes without knowing it. That is because you need to start fighting with the gifts that were afforded to you. There are many gifts but they are all of the same Spirit which is God. There are differences of administration, but the same Lord. Christians are to perform executive duties. When you are an executive you don't behave in the same manner as everyone else around you. There is a certain dignity that you uphold yourself to. We are always to be a light for God. We are not of the world we just live in the world. For it to be stated that the spiritual gifts are not available right now is a mystery in and of itself. If this is denied but yet we still say that we have the word of knowledge and wisdom. We are scared of the concept of the spiritual gifts because certain people lack or don't have these gifts. This doesn't mean that the gifts are not in our midst. They were not given to us only for those of old. These gifts are still among us and if we would search them out without condemning the person that has been given the gifts and try to nurture and assist the individuals who are able to help the Church of Christ with growth and other issues that are plaguing us as well as the community. The Church as a whole will condemn this person and call them evil or even tell them that they ate something that they shouldn't have. We will make up something because of the fear that we have allowed to seep into our home. The pastors will go to these scriptures and pull out the ones that they are comfortable with and speak on those and leave the rest of the meat on the bone. This is not to bash anyone this is only for the knowledge of those that God has placed these marvelous gifts. Some of our churches are listening and assisting the members that are gifted and trying to help the individuals understand what is happening and why it is happening. To those churches I want to thank you. There are not many but there are some. Every good and perfect thing comes from God. It is a great thing to be able to tell someone what you see for them in the spirit. The people that we speak to may not appreciate it at that moment but eventually they will try to get an understanding of what was stated to them. You are not sent to convince nor convict them your job is only to speak what the spirit gives you to say to them. God will handle the rest. I am able to prophesy and am allowing the Holy Spirit to guide me to speak in tongue. Speaking in an unknown tongue (speaking to God) 1 Corinthians 14:2For he that speaketh in an unknown tongue speaketh not unto men, but unto God: for no man understandeth him; howbeit in the spirit he speaketh mysteries. Is solely an experience of words that you may not understand but He has placed them in your spirit for you to speak to Him. Know that you are not crazy. There is a God and He knows what He is doing. Don't let anyone discourage you no matter who it may be. God gave you something that no man can take away from you and you have it for a reason. I fought writing this book because I didn't want to lose my families support and love. But God, but God that is all I can say. God has placed me inside the belly of the whale. I am laughing at this moment because I have been helping people get out of the whale or stay away from the whale that I saw approaching them and I myself had an epiphany that I am in the whale myself. That is funny. I am going to help you as much as I can. This is truly through the inspiration of God. We do have spiritual gifts they are not gone, didn't die out, nor do they cost anything. NO you are not crazy! NO, you didn't eat something that didn't agree with you! And, NO, you are not evil by any means! It is time for us to stop feeling like we have to answer to anyone besides God because God has blessed you. It is time for us to stop pushing this gift into a place of nothingness a place of suppression because no one understands what we are going through because we just like them don't know what is going on. I am blessed to have some wonderful people enter into my life all of my life and explain things that I may have not known. If you ask God to help you I am here to tell you that He will. He will place individuals around you to bring you to the knowledge of whatever gift(s) He has placed in you. We are going to be alright because Jesus is coming back for His church and the people on this earth don't have the key to your salvation nor can they speak to Him and talk ill of you. You are the captain of your fate. Don't feel ashamed or bad to use your spiritual gifts to do the will of God. God gave you that gift for a reason. I know some of you have seen or felt something that should have been spoken to someone around you and you didn't do it because you didn't want them to say that you were doing witchcraft or you didn't want to feel uncomfortable because they were going to tell the pastor what you were saying. Some of you have hands that are able to heal those around you. If you think back to certain great instances when you were younger when you didn't care about what the adults were saying when someone wasn't feeling well or someone was bleeding and you would touch them and they would feel better or they would stop bleeding you felt great. You didn't think you were the bomb you just felt great. Take a moment and think. I know there were many instances that I would be outside playing and a cousin or sibling would fall down and they would come running to me to touch them so they would stop bleeding. They would say " She is going to be a doctor when she gets older". It is funny because I never really understood what was going on. We as members of the body of Christ need to grasp hold of these great things that have already manifested in our lives. We are in the right place to be and when you take hold of the greatness of God and not worry about what the others are saying you will see what He has available for you. You may be having visions of greatness just sitting there around you and you are doing everything that the Word has instructed you to do but you are not getting to that place where God keeps showing you that He wants you to be. You may be frustrated or you may have just learned to settle like the rest of the people around you. God has given you a dream that you want to see manifest. You may be crying out to God and telling the Father I am and have done everything where is the manifestation of this dream? I am here to tell you that God is saying "My child I told you to touch that child and heal them, I told you to tell that child to watch the company that they are keeping, I told you to tell that mother to stay away from that man, I told you not to go to that place, I told you…, I told you…, I told you… I am waiting for you to do what I told you." It is time for us to get out of comfortable and get into awesome. It is time for us to do the WILL OF GOD and not the will of man. No good and perfect thing will be held back when you do the Will of God. This is meaning something to someone. God doesn't do ordinary He does extraordinary if you let Him! Step out on faith the next time you feel your spirit jumping and you have something to do thus says the Lord and watch Him show out in your life. Furthermore, the denial of these great gifts is keeping us at a division as well as denying the Spirit of God. Matthew 12:32 clearly states that if we deny the Holy Ghost it shall not be forgiven us. When we deny the gifts that God has given to us we deny the Holy Ghost. We are essentially denying God no matter how you try to sugar coat the issue. A house divided is not able to stand. Matthew 12:25 every kingdom divided against itself is brought to desolation. If this is not dividing the kingdom of God I don't know what is. This is a great division among the saints. It is sad and now it is time for change. Most of us are waking up and not pleasing man but God. I am doing the Will of my Father. You can get mad and scandalize my name but God…. But God…. 1 John 2: 20But ye have an unction from the Holy One, and ye know all things. Through the Holy Spirit you are able to use spiritual gifts to see into your right now, future, and past. You are able to be guided to do what God wants done for His kingdom. He wants to use you to bring about His work in the world. Why is that so hard for us to see? Because we allow the enabler to enable us by placing a cloud of doubt from the naysayers, we don't want them to say anything negative about us. We have an image to sustain. "They are not going to want to be around us anymore. I am going to be by myself." Newsflash when you die, you die and are going to be judged by God by yourself. There is an anointing that abides in you it is just waiting for you to grab it and use it. 1 John 2: 27But the anointing which ye have received of him abideth in you, and ye need not that any man teach you: but as the same anointing teacheth you of all things, and is truth, and is no lie, and even as it hath taught you, ye shall abide in him. The anointing is going to give you utterance as you ask for direction. The Spirit searches all things and reveals them unto us as the Spirit has the revelation from the Spirit of God. What is in your spirit is not understood by your flesh you must be spiritual and not carnal. While you are telling people how God will bless you as you have had dreams or visions about there may be a carnal minded person that will ask you how and have you doubting what God is doing in your life. Don't doubt. The Holy Spirit is here to give instruction to the Purpose People. This will become activated in you are you in the Will of God. We are to be led by the Spirit don't be led by others opinions of how they see you. We have all seen things that we thought were horrid because we were on the outside looking in but as we have had time to investigate the circumstances are not as grave as we perceived.

There are many that are looking at my situation and they are feeling sorry for me they are not looking with the Spirit but looking carnally. God has shown me what is awaiting me as I walk in the Spirit. I am led by the Spirit. Romans 8: 14For as many as are led by the Spirit of God, they are the sons of God. I am trying to receive everything that God has for me. Gifts of the Holy Spirit will bring forth the fullness of His ministry in your life we are allowed to minister effectively one to another and to help bring to pass God's Will in the earth. John 14: 12Verily, verily, I say unto you, He that believeth on me, the works that I do shall he do also; and greater works than these shall he do; because I go unto my Father. I believe in Him. I know what He said He did He did. I wasn't there but I know that it is said thus says the Lord so it is right. If you believe it states that you to will be able to do what Jesus came here to do and do things greater in your works. I didn't say that the word has stated this. You have to be a steward of the Holy Spirit because if He lives dormant in you then it is not to the Glory of God. 1 Peter 4: 10As every man hath received the gift, even so minister the same one to another, as good stewards of the manifold grace of God. Every man has the Holy Spirit. The gifts are manifest with purpose, in the proper time, and in the proper place. Some of us have Wisdom this is the Wisdom of God. 1 Corinthians 6: 6-9 6Howbeit we speak wisdom among them that are perfect: yet not the wisdom of this world, nor of the princes of this world, that come to nought: 7But we speak the wisdom of God in a mystery, even the hidden wisdom, which God ordained before the world unto our glory: 8Which none of the princes of this world knew: for had they known it, they would not have crucified the Lord of glory. 9But as it is written, Eye hath not seen, nor ear heard, neither have entered into the heart of man, the things which God hath prepared for them that love him. 10But God hath revealed them unto us by his Spirit: for the Spirit searcheth all things, yea, the deep things of God. 11For what man knoweth the things of a man, save the spirit of man which is in him? even so the things of God knoweth no man, but the Spirit of God. 12Now we have received, not the spirit of the world, but the spirit which is of God; that we might know the things that are freely given to us of God. 13Which things also we speak, not in the words which man's wisdom teacheth, but which the Holy Ghost teacheth; comparing spiritual things with spiritual. 14But the natural man receiveth not the things of the Spirit of God: for they are foolishness unto him: neither can he know them, because they are spiritually discerned. 15But he that is spiritual judgeth all things, yet he himself is judged of no man. 16For who hath known the mind of the Lord, that he may instruct him? but we have the mind of Christ. Your wisdom is coming from God through the Holy Spirit. Those that have this wisdom know that there is nothing that you can say that will get them out of the Will of God. They know that what God has said He was going to do He is going to do it in His time. Those that have wisdom the wisdom of God will see you going through something and tell you to hold on and tell you to "Praise God because He is about to do something. He is getting you ready for a supernatural blessing a blessing that is only coming from Him" Most of us are moments away from this wise person this person for most of us is our grandmother or grandfather. When they pray out and their prayer is answered they know how to reach out in travail and beg for the change that they know is needed in our lives so we are able to be in a position to do it for ourselves and most importantly so that we are in the place of worship to get to Heaven. They don't want to see us going in the other direction which only leads to pain and torture. Travail produces spiritual children for as soon as Zion travailed she brought forth her children Isaiah 66:8 Paul was a man of travail Galatians 4: 19My little children, of whom I travail in birth again until Christ be formed in you. Paul was a wise man. The wise are few in number because many of the Christians in our services now are forgetting to act Christlike. Colossians 24Who now rejoice in my sufferings for you, and fill up that which is behind of the afflictions of Christ in my flesh for his body's sake, which is the church: We have to suffer to get to a place of spiritual comfort with God. If we don't then the carnal being in us will again take over. There are many different forms that travail may take and varying depths of pain involved. Some of these are mild sensations of heaviness or depression, or just the general feeling of a burden. Some people weep, cry, moan, or groan. Others even experience symptoms like birth pains or heart pains while in deep travail. One can experience any of these feelings separately or in combination. You can all but guarantee these wise people have been in a form of travail on several instances concerning you or someone that you know. You may even be the person that is the wise one that has gone through such travail. Whichever you are most people travail in private and people that are not in the Spirit don't and won't understand what I am speaking about. Those that have been in travail know what I am speaking of. This is just food for thought. There are many instances of travail in the Word: Daniel 7:15I Daniel was grieved in my spirit in the midst of my body, and the visions of my head troubled me. In this instance Daniel had troubled visions so he went into a form of travail we soon read that his travail was answered. Daniel 7: 16I came near unto one of them that stood by, and asked him the truth of all this. So he told me, and made me know the interpretation of the things. Daniel 8:27And I Daniel fainted, and was sick certain days; afterward I rose up, and did the king's business; and I was astonished at the vision, but none understood it. Read Daniel he travailed a lot. In Hannah travailed for a child and was given a child. 1 Samuel 1:5-18 5But unto Hannah he gave a worthy portion; for he loved Hannah: but the LORD had shut up her womb. 6And her adversary also provoked her sore, for to make her fret, because the LORD had shut up her womb. 7And as he did so year by year, when she went up to the house of the LORD, so she provoked her; therefore she wept, and did not eat. 8Then said Elkanah her husband to her, Hannah, why weepest thou? and why eatest thou not? and why is thy heart grieved? am not I better to thee than ten sons? 9So Hannah rose up after they had eaten in Shiloh, and after they had drunk. Now Eli the priest sat upon a seat by a post of the temple of the LORD. 10And she was in bitterness of soul, and prayed unto the LORD, and wept sore. 11And she vowed a vow, and said, O LORD of hosts, if thou wilt indeed look on the affliction of thine handmaid, and remember me, and not forget thine handmaid, but wilt give unto thine handmaid a man child, then I will give him unto the LORD all the days of his life, and there shall no razor come upon his head. 12And it came to pass, as she continued praying before the LORD, that Eli marked her mouth. 13Now Hannah, she spake in her heart; only her lips moved, but her voice was not heard: therefore Eli thought she had been drunken. 14And Eli said unto her, How long wilt thou be drunken? put away thy wine from thee. 15And Hannah answered and said, No, my lord, I am a woman of a sorrowful spirit: I have drunk neither wine nor strong drink, but have poured out my soul before the LORD. 16Count not thine handmaid for a daughter of Belial: for out of the abundance of my complaint and grief have I spoken hitherto. 17Then Eli answered and said, Go in peace: and the God of Israel grant thee thy petition that thou hast asked of him. 18And she said, Let thine handmaid find grace in thy sight. So the woman went her way, and did eat, and her countenance was no more sad. Jeremiah it is sad that the men were travailing like women! Jeremiah 30: 5-6 For thus saith the LORD; We have heard a voice of trembling, of fear, and not of peace. 6Ask ye now, and see whether a man doth travail with child? wherefore do I see every man with his hands on his loins, as a woman in travail, and all faces are turned into paleness? Travail brings answers and some freedom from many issues that are plaguing us. Jesus was also in travail for Lazarus because He was bringing him back. John 11: 35Jesus wept. He also travailed in the Garden of Gethsemane; Luke 22: 41And he was withdrawn from them about a stone's cast, and kneeled down, and prayed, 42Saying, Father, if thou be willing, remove this cup from me: nevertheless not my will, but thine, be done. 43And there appeared an angel unto him from heaven, strengthening him. 44And being in an agony he prayed more earnestly: and his sweat was as it were great drops of blood falling down to the ground. If this in and of itself doesn't give you strength to inhabit the Will of God then I don't know what to tell you. We experience deliverance as we cry and travail for others and ourselves. Travailing is yielding to the sorrow of God's heart over a situation. Travailing praying is a mighty spiritual weapon. There is also the gift of knowledge in which is the ability to have an in-depth understanding with spiritual issues and/or situations people that can look at what you are going through and give you insight that you would have not come to on your own. They are so full of the word when they speak you know they are correct. They have Bible knowledge. This person can look into all of the foolishness that you may have been placing yourself through and see that you are trying to come out as the head and not the tail but there is something holding you back you are not letting something go that God wants to be gone so He can use you. They will see exactly what it is and tell you exactly what the Wisdom of God is speaking and tell it in a way that you don't get upset you start into a travail that will break the yoke that is holding onto everything that you are trying to become. We are also blessed with discernment (common sense) the ability to determine whether a message, person, or event is truly from God. They sense things in the spirit and know what is good or not in the spirit. They know if something is genuine or fake. We will take information to this person to get their point of view of the situation. To make sure we are making the right decision or if we should just leave the situation alone. For the most part you don't even have to bring this individual your situation they are going to sense it and speak on it anyway. They know that they are doing God's Will and it is for you to use what they are telling you. We are constantly fighting against our flesh and the fight will not be won if we don't get our flesh under subjection with our spirit. All spiritual gifts manifest right purpose, place, and time. There are power gifts that are also spiritual gifts there are those of us that have faith that no matter what comes in their path they have the faith and the ability to trust God and encourage others to trust God no matter the circumstances. There are those that work in miracles they have the ability to perform signs and wonders that give authentication to God's word. The gift of healing is the one of those. The miraculous ability to utilize God's healing power to restore a person that is sick. It is not your power it is His healing power. You have to be careful with this gift because you may get besides yourself and think that it is you and that a healing will only happen if you are there. If the person is not healed it is not because they didn't have faith. It may not have been the Will of God. They may have been healed in other ways. We have to die of something if He doesn't heal you still bless His name. Vocal gifts of tongues you will have the ability to speak in a foreign language that you do not have knowledge of in order to communicate with someone who speaks that language. Real tongues are traced to a language. Don't mix that up with speaking in an unknown tongue speaking with God there is no way to trace that language and it is an intimate conversation with God that not even the enemy is able to translate what you are saying. 1 Corinthians 14:2For he that speaketh in an unknown tongue speaketh not unto men, but unto God: for no man understandeth him; howbeit in the spirit he speaketh mysteries. The gift of interpretation you are able to hear the tongue and tell what the other

person is speaking based on the Word of God.
Prophesy the message of God in proclamation.
And the greatest of them all is love no matter what
gift you have if you don't have love it means
nothing. All these gifts move together for the Will
of God

Heavenly Father I ask that You enhance every spiritual gift
that is laying dormant in me right now. Lord I ask that
You send people to me that will assist in the awakening and
who have the knowledge to show me what I need to know to
use these gifts. Father, I ask that You give me courage to
use these gifts as needed and that they are an asset to many.
Father, I ask that You give me the wisdom to fight this
fight and the strength to endure every ridicule that comes my
way. Please send Your ministering angels to assist me while
I am weeping so that they give me the strength and the
courage that I need to stop. Align my ear with Your graces
so that I may hear the angels. Let my spiritual eye be open

to see the angels let me be so tuned with Your Word. Help me to search the scriptures every day and night to show myself approved. Move those people and places out of my life that are hindering my spiritual growth. Father help me to become stronger and help me to realize that it is not my will but Thy Will.

In the name of Jesus I pray

Amen.

Chapter 2

Are You Special?

Are you special? I have had to deal with this issue all of my life. Not directly. But in the sermons that I have had to listen to when they feel they are being led to condemn those that have let go and let God. They are speaking about something that they have not yet understood because no one is speaking out in the Church of Christ. I do feel that it is a great blessing for these gifts. Almost every Sunday I hear the minister speaking and asking the congregation "if they can do all these things can they raise the dead?" I have not seen anyone raise the dead nor have I but I know that there is nothing impossible for God to perform through you. But they will attack the premise of the spiritual gift by saying that "God doesn't respect any man". I think they condemn the whole concept of the greatness of having the gifts so much this is where the fear sets in. Most of us attend church with our family and friends. They are in a circle so tight sometimes that it is hard to really try to get an understanding of who you can speak to concerning the changes you may be experiencing. Get on your knees and speak to God. You don't want to seem as if you feel you are special because, it is wrong to be special. Is it? When we look at those that are special they had to do things that set them apart from others around them. Everyone that God used in the Bible there was something that set them apart from the rest. They were the youngest, smaller, swore more, like to be nude, had big personalities, had no personality, lost husbands, etc. Mostly everyone that was spoken about had something different going on and they may have been ashamed of the difference but God gave them what they needed to get the job done so He got the glory for whatever the situation may have been. Look at Moses he didn't feel he could talk right so he was given assistance. He could have done it on his own but he didn't believe in himself. So he didn't want to do it because he didn't feel special. Jonah didn't want to go and speak to the city of Nineveh because he just knew in his heart of hearts that they wouldn't listen and when they did that really set him on fire. He didn't feel that the people were special. He felt that was a waste of his time. Sometimes when you are delivering the Word many will not receive it right at that moment and really some not at all it is not up to us to hold the word back from the person or people that are supposed to receive it. God may have sent you as a confirmation to that person or you may be the first one to deliver the message. Your job only is to deliver the message the reasoning and all behind it is for God to give to the person you are speaking. You are special in your own way. We are all special. We are all unique because we are not made the same. Does that not in and of itself make us special? We are members of the Church of Christ? We are set apart from the world by Christ that makes us special. There are so many diverse ways we are different so we are indeed special. Don't allow this question to make you feel that you are higher than anyone to attempt to make you want to belittle yourself. God thinks something of you for whatever His reasons are. Find strength in Him and His word and not the words of man. Man has neither a Heaven nor Hell for any of us to go. In my opinion yes, you are special because you are one of a few that have decided to open up your eyes concerning the awesome things that God is able to do. He can do it all. You are special because you know and have seen the greatness of God. You know that God is able. You are special because Matthew 7:14 speaks to us informing us that only the special are going to enter because there are only a few there be that find the entrance.

You are special because you realize the urgency needed in the Churches of Christ to understand and to assist the world in the deliverance of God's people. There are some that will speak and tell you that God isn't a respecter of any man. Because you have these spiritual gifts this is not saying that you have God's respect it is saying that God wants to use you. You are His vessel. Many that were used did want to be used but eventually they learned to let go and let God. You are not perfect but you are able to understand (maybe not right now but if you ask Him He will show you) the spiritual gifts that are bestowed to you. You are only borrowing the gifts because there will come a time when we will not be able to use the gifts so while they are available to us as Christians doesn't it make sense to ask for the gifts to edify your congregation? If you see the destruction of a members child or a family member or someone that is not doing the right things or maybe they are doing the right things but they are still not getting to the place that God wants them don't you feel special because you are able to speak the words that God has given to you to this person? Now it will feel great to do this without feeling like you are doing something wrong because you won't have to sneak to do it. God didn't give you this to sneak and tell anyone anything. He didn't give this to you for you to tell someone what thus says the Lord and then end it with don't tell anyone that I told you. That is not why you are blessed it is not a curse to have a spiritual gift it is a blessing. There is no place in the bible where it says that when Jesus died and rose again that we are not still blessed with spiritual gifts. You are special because you realize this. It states that in the Old Testament that there were no open visions before this but now we are blessed with open vision. You are special because you now know that it is okay and that you are responsible for development through meditation, prayer and study. You are special because you realize The Holy Spirit gives these gifts as they are needed and seeing that the first gifts mentioned are word of wisdom and knowledge one might think that every Christian should pray especially for these gifts. Wisdom and knowledge would allow us to know how to use any other gifts which we might be given If you ask for helpers you will receive helpers. I prayed for people to be placed around me that were conscious to the spiritual gifts. If you pray for these people to be placed around you they will show up. No sooner than I prayed for someone to even help me with my prayers to God the person showed up. No sooner than I asked God for spiritual gift guides they showed up. I am not by any means telling that the road that you are about to go down is going to be easy. It is not! To whom much is given much is required. You are going to be ridiculed by the best and the worst of them. This is something new to many in our church and if it is something that many of them can't do they are going to betray you and try to hinder you from getting it done. Pray for strength as you go through. While each of our great pioneers of something different were going through and getting to their destiny they cried out to the Lord in prayer and song. Reach out when you need it. We are all special to our creator because we have a special cause in the manifestation of His Will. You have to be careful with your gifts though because you have to deal with people that may be a little jealous of your gifts as a prophet in 1 Kings had to learn with his life. When God tells you something you have to listen and do as He tells you to do. Others are not always looking out for your best interest. God may say to go some place just this once and speak this to this person just this once. Don't let your flesh take over and then you go and speak more than once. You have to do what thus says the Lord. Hebrews

13: 5Let your conversation be without covetousness; and be content with such things as ye have: for he hath said, I will never leave thee, nor forsake thee. God is telling us once again that we are special in His eyes. He will never leave us we leave Him. You are special because you are blessed due to your belief. Luke 1:

45And blessed is she that believed: for there shall be a performance of those things which were told her from the Lord. I don't know about you but I have read the word for myself and there are many things that have been told to me by my Lord. I believe and I shall receive. Mark 11:24 Therefore I say unto you, What things soever ye desire, when ye pray, believe that ye receive them, and ye shall have them. It is in you to believe you just have to be delivered from the limitation that we as a culture have dared to place on God. God made everything and has placed everything at our feet. When you go outside and look up into what we perceive to be heaven and you look at the beautiful sky and see all the wonders all around you He created all of that and you. Look and thank Him. Man didn't make anything the material things that are placed here that are good and perfect those too came from Him. Every great, good, and perfect idea that you have had have come from Him. He didn't have to save you from anything He did it because He loves us. Why are we afraid to show Him that we love Him? You don't show Him when you are living in fear and when you are letting man dictate what spiritual gifts are still here and which ones are gone. Could it be that they are in denial because the one that is special is not steeping out and letting Him direct your path. He never leads you into a place that was not comfortable for long, or that was unsafe for you to travel, or you were not going to be delivered! 1 Corinthians 1: 31That, according as it is written, He that glorieth, let him glory in the Lord. *Father, help* me to see that there is something special in me. You created us all in Your image and no one is the same as another even twins are different. Father, give me courage on today to fight the good fight of faith help me to walk securely down this road to glory. I know that it is not going to be easy and I also know that if it were easy it would not be appreciated. Father, help me to appreciate Your presence in my life. Guide me through every avenue of my life. Remove the obstacles that are hindering me from reaching the destiny that You have for me. Lord, give me strength while You are removing the obstacles that are hindering me in my journey of being a delegated warrior in Your fight for balance in our churches. Father, the blood of Jesus was shed so that we are able to make changes for the better in our lives if He hadn't died for us so many of us would not be here now. Father, I thank You for the blood of Jesus. Jesus as you are mediating for me I thank You I know sometimes You may want to snap crackle and pop me I thank You that you don't I thank You that You see something special in me

and that You love me more than I love myself. Teach me
how to be more like You. Let me be a special Christian
and let others see the change that is occurring in my life.
In the name of Jesus
Amen

Chapter 3

Speaking in Tongue

1 Corinthians 14 1Follow after charity, and desire spiritual gifts, but rather that ye may prophesy. 2For he that speaketh in an unknown tongue speaketh not unto men, but unto God: for no man understandeth him; howbeit in the spirit he speaketh mysteries. 3But he that prophesieth speaketh unto men to edification, and exhortation, and comfort. 4He that speaketh in an unknown tongue edifieth himself; but he that prophesieth edifieth the church. 5I would that ye all spake with tongues but rather that ye prophesied: for greater is he that prophesieth than he that speaketh with tongues, except he

interpret, that the church may receive edifying.

6Now, brethren, if I come unto you speaking with tongues, what shall I profit you, except I shall speak to you either by revelation, or by knowledge, or by prophesying, or by doctrine? 7And even things without life giving sound, whether pipe or harp, except they give a distinction in the sounds, how shall it be known what is piped or harped? 8For if the trumpet give an uncertain sound, who shall prepare himself to the battle? 9So likewise ye, except ye utter by the tongue words easy to be understood, how shall it be known what is spoken? for ye shall speak into the air. 10There are, it may be, so many kinds of voices in the world, and none of them is without signification. 11Therefore if I know not the meaning of the voice, I shall be unto him that speaketh a barbarian, and he that speaketh shall be a barbarian unto me. 12Even so ye, forasmuch as ye are zealous of spiritual gifts, seek that ye may excel to the edifying of the church.

Examine 1 Corinthians 14: 1-12 we see that these gifts are desired after charity. Now you have to desire spiritual gifts. Speaking in tongue is a spiritual gift. Speaking in tongue is speaking a language that is known to a community of people as their dialect. There are those that are able to communicate with just making differing noises to each other and that is their means of communication because you are not able to understand what is being said doesn't mean that the information is obsolete. There are organizations and different missionaries that will seek out to learn the language that is being spoken by these individuals as well as the origin of the language. In our society many individuals will start speaking language to keep those around them from understanding what is being communicated by them. We take the time to understand. One such group in America is our teenagers. Our teenagers speak to each other and have come up with a language to be spoken both on the internet and on the phone through texting and speaking. Because this has become an unsafe act because pedophiles have taken on the language and understood what was being said and they even tried to help with the development in this language so they can make our children feel uncomfortable and misunderstood at home and eventually want to leave from our homes. This unknown language has become known due to the efforts of many organizations and the police. There are also other instances of new languages coming about with the good ole Pig Latin, and Ebonics. We didn't except these languages either but it was a form of communication that caused issues for families around the world so they were things that had to be learned. People try to find many ways to communicate in a mission impossible way. There are things that they don't want everyone to know. So why is it not possible for the language that is being spoken in some churches as a language? Yes it may be something that you don't understand because you have not asked for the understanding. I was so about to just write that this is just speaking a language that is known by a community. Indeed it is. We are becoming so divided for silly things. The human race is very articulate and extremely intelligent. Why are we placing a value on what is being stated by whomever is speaking? This is not stating that there shouldn't be anyone there to interpret what is being said. There has to be someone around to understand what is being said or the person should be quiet. A lot of our preachers like I stated are scared of this gift because they don't know what to do with the people that are speaking and they don't understand what is being said. The preacher is responsible for the teaching of the saints and the saints are responsible to go out into the world and preach, demonstrate, and manifest the gospel. It is the responsibility of the church to make the devil behave. We can't do that if we are denying the gifts that He has given us to be used to fight the devil because they were not taught. The gifts are manifest with the interpretation of the utterance of what you are able to handle without fear. You can't be afraid of what God wants to do in your life. There is a level of edification that comes along with the gifts. We are lights for others and as being lights for others we are living our lives as ensamples of Christ right? So while we are striving to do better we are getting better and God is giving us these spiritual gifts. For the most part I only can speak for what I know. These gifts are already within you and many of us have had to suppress these gifts so we have the ignoring them down. But as you grow in the Word of God your spiritual you is also growing so is that awesome gift that God is giving you. For those of us that have stuck it out we know that there is no other place for us to be because we are trying to make it to Heaven. We are learning how to use these gifts and help others on the low low. These are the ones that I am speaking to right now. There are so many of our children and the children of others that are going through what you have already had to deal with. Trying to keep this gift quiet and it is not fair! Your child or someone around you has spoken to you and told you that they had a dream about something that is happening to them right now. When you are speaking in tongue you are speaking to God as well as edifying the Church. When did the edification of the church end in the Word? I don't see where it states that it was ended. The ones that don't believe will say that it ended when Jesus died and rose again. Examine 1 Corinthians 14: 1-12 we see that these gifts are desired after charity. Now you have to desire spiritual gifts. There is a war going on everybody. Stop letting the enemy divide and conquer help each other. It is really a sad thing to see all of this going on. To the believers there is nothing wrong with us. The Church is growing and Jesus is coming back with the embrace of everything that He has given us. If we cannot accept all of what He has placed here how are we going to embrace all the wonderful and awesome things that are waiting for us? We don't want to say "hallelujah" in service what is going on with that? Don't let "Sister Silky" say it loud the conservative bunch will look at her so evil. That person knows what is going on. We have become so conservative. Not saying the highest praise of them all. Hello. 1 Corinthians 14:18 - I thank my God, I speak with tongues more than you all. The apostle says, to observe to them that he did not despise speaking with tongues: nor did he attempt to conquer the use of their gifts. He didn't attempt to discourage them from desiring them. He didn't envy their having them. He also was blessed with them himself. His gifts were very distinguished and he made use of his gifts. He could speak with more tongues than any of those that had them, and spoke them often. Utilizing them through his travel into different countries while preaching the Gospel to people of divers languages. He mentions this not in a boasting manner, but in great humility, giving thanks to God, and acknowledging him to be the author of this gift. So speaking in tongue is speaking in different languages as well as speaking with God in the unknown tongue. We are afforded the opportunity to speak to others in their tongue by learning their language. They were blessed because they were just able to know what was being said and speak in the tongue by the grace of God through the Holy Spirit. There was a time when I was younger that I was able to understand what people were saying while shopping with my mother for instance when I was younger we were in a Chinese hair store and there was a husband and wife in the shop speaking to each other I understood everything that they were saying. I was so in tuned with that ability because I didn't have anyone telling me that I couldn't because I was not supposed to. If we stop placing this unfounded display of doubt on each other and start watching out for these things this to can still be done. I remember the husband looking at me and telling his wife that I could understand what they were saying. I have been praying for that ability to be able to understand and to speak without the study of the languages this is what speaking in tongues is speaking without the study of the language. I know that God can do it I just have to have faith. Pray for me. Watch your children when you are walking through places where they are speaking another language ask them if they understand what is being said. While doing this don't alarm them in any manner. I guarantee you there will be a surprise coming your way. I wish I would have told my mother then. I didn't know what was going on because we don't talk about this at home nor at church. I am not sure as to how she could have assisted me. If you are able to see this for yourself pray that God will send you some assistance into how to handle this. Back to the other side of the coin when you are able to get your church or your family on one accord with this remember this verse: 1 Corinthians 14:23 "If therefore the whole church be come together into one place, and all speak with tongues, and there come in *those that are* unlearned, or unbelievers, will they not say that you are mad?" You know how people act when they feel something is wrong with you. They tend to stay away from you. Don't worry and don't fret. God will move those that don't belong around you away from you. Everyone is not going to understand or want to learn more of who God is. The idea is that the church would usually speak the same language with the people were they live and if they made use of foreign languages which were incomprehensible to their visitors it would leave the notion that the church was in a pandemonium. Some who don't believe and many that do believe while placing a limitation on what God can and does perform. We as Christians need to stop doubting the ability of God. You may feel inferior or uncertain. You may feel that this is improper in our congregations. Many will feel led to abstain from the use of such language in worship. Please don't forget as Paul warns if no one interprets or no one understands the language, keep silent. That is why it is a crucial situation to find out who is able to perform what spiritual gift in your surroundings. Speaking in tongue is a language that is already here that a community utilizes to communicate between one another. The Hip Hop community has started its own language and has a dictionary so that others are able to understand this language.

Father, You are the beginning and the end alpha and omega. Give me the courage to continue as the enemy wants me to think that it is getting harder and harder. Father, I bind the enemy in my life around and about me. I ask that on today every obstacle is removed from my path the seen and unseen known and unknown obstacles are gone. Father, I ask that You show me what is needed from me on today. Lord, give me courage to use the gifts that are given to me openly and that You protect me from those that will try to *abuse me to get at my gift to destroy me. Give me the wisdom that is needed with this gift. Show me how to acquire discernment and how to use it in my everyday life.* Place courage so deeply within me so I am able to continue this fight as I am ridiculed for believing in what Your Word says. Lord, Your word tells me that I am able to have spiritual gifts and that I have to ask for them I have already asked Lord now show me how and when to use them teach me Your ways I want to be with You in the end. I want Your glory to shine brighter than anything that I have ever seen. I want to be a shining light for Your people. Everyone may walk away from me I am not here to please them I am here for Your glory God. Help me as I continue. In the name of Jesus

Amen

Chapter 4

Speaking with God

We are speaking an unknown language when we are speaking to God. There is a misconception that this is not happening that this is just jibber jabber. There is no way to know what the person is speaking because it is unknown to those that are hearing it.

1 Corinthians 14:2 For he that speaketh in an unknown tongue speaketh not unto men, but unto God: for no man understandeth him; howbeit in the spirit he speaketh mysteries.

We essentially doubt that God is able to do anything. It clearly states that the individual is speaking to God and not man. I believe that because the church is in such denial most of the leadership has not subjected them totally to the Will of God in that manner. What I mean by that is that they have not believed that God is still allowing us to utilize the gift of speaking to Him in a manner that no one else is able to understand because the relationship has become so intimate with Him. No one else needs to know what you are saying to the Father. This is just as if you are speaking with your earthly parent and you don't want anyone else knowing what you have said to that parent. You only want the person you are speaking with to know what you are dealing with and how you are dealing with it. Rather it is good, bad, or ugly. You want the advice that they are able to give you but you don't want this information uttered to anyone else and let's face it no matter what earthly person you speak your most intimate detail to they are going to speak it to someone else and they are not able to fix the problem. The only individual that you can and should trust is God. When you speak to Him the issue is resolved with His assistance whether He does it all Himself or gives you the path to walk to remove the obstacles out of your path. The Father has all the answers. My grandmother has always said "if you don't want anyone else to know your secret keep it to yourself." The person that you are speaking to also has someone that they feel comfortable speaking to and they will speak it to someone else. It may not always be meant for them to speak it sometimes they may have a oops. When you speak to the Author and Finisher of the Word then you are speaking to someone that is able to finish everything that has been started. When you let go and let God there are so many awesome experiences that will be open unto us. There are many instances that we will be made aware of once we take the block off the communication with God. Yes, there is a block. The block is what we feel is impossible to God.

There is nothing impossible for Him to perform in our lives. He can and will do it all. You have to get out of your comfort zone and walk while holding on. He has shown us on so many different instances that He is God and He can do it if we just believe. Faith is what? The Hebrew writer tells us in Hebrews 11 that faith is the substance of things hoped for, the evidence of things not seen. So we as a church need to hope for some miracles and wait for the manifestation of the greatness of God. When we have someone we love fighting a battle we will hope for a miracle. While we are hoping for that miracle we are watching as the manifestation for them is complete. So many folks have been in and out of the hospital for surgery or just not knowing. I know what God has said to me through His Word which was made flesh and dwelt among us. I know that through my faith(hope) and my prayers that things are going to happen. My uncle and my grandfather have been in the hospital I know for a fact that my uncle was fearful of coming out of his surgery alive. He was so frightened that he called my grandmother and voiced that to her. God had already showed me that he was going to be alright so I was not fearful. I told her that he was going to be alright because God wasn't done with him yet. I don't let anyone take what I know that God is showing me or telling me. It feels awesome to know that you know that you know. When God gives you something when he is ministering to you don't let anyone take that away from you and replace it with doubt. When you are in the midst of something great and you know that God is for you don't let anyone speak to you otherwise. Stay away from the doubters. The doubters will have you sinking deep in sin because you are not believing what the King of Kings is telling you. When He is speaking to you and no one believes what He is saying to you keep it to yourself. He didn't give the information to them he gave it to you. Now it is time for you to talk to God and pray your obstacles out of the way. You don't have to know what these obstacles are He knows so you ask Him to remove them. Don't be afraid you have already been speaking with God this is just a closer communion with the Father. This is your 911 page you heard me. No one is knowing what you are saying to Him but Him. That in and of itself is the greatest thing ever you have already been speaking with Him while you are praying you are speaking to Him. There may be some comments that you left out or you may not have been comfortable saying. The enemy doesn't even know what you are saying when you are speaking in tongue! If that is not the most awesome tool to use to get your words to Him and only Him please believe there are going to be many that are going to be jealous because they have not let go and let the glory of Jesus shine in on them. There are going to be so many awesome things that are going to happen to you as you go through this journey. You need not be scared and you need not speak them to everyone due to everyone not knowing what to tell you and the jealousy factor. The only one that you need to be speaking with more closely is the Lord. If there is something that you are not able to understand who better to answer your questions. God will give you the answer to whatever question you have and the only payment He wants is for you to act right. You can't buy Him at any store. Your family and friends can say whatever they desire they will in no way change how He feels about you. You speak to God and ask for the utterance you need to speak to Him walk down the path that only leads to His door. Speak and be delivered out of what you are going through. Speak and help someone else that is in dire need. Speak and watch how things are going to turn around every place you step your foot in. While you are speaking make sure you are listening to what He is saying. Get a handy dandy notebook and keep one by your bed, in the car, and at work. There is not a set time for your answer. He may respond immediately or not. Whenever He answers it is always on time. There will be times when you will receive the answer in a dream. We all know what happens most times when you are getting up most of us will forget what we dreamed about. Has nothing to do with age. The enemy doesn't want you to remember because that is going to bring remedy to something or someone. As soon as you get up write it down. Don't even get out of the bed have the pad and pen in arms reach and get to writing. I had a dream about this man that God has told me is my husband. I have dreamed about this individual so much I had finally started enjoying the facet of marriage once again. Then I had a dream about him with someone else I had read a book the day before about what God has for you it is for you but sometimes He wants to see if you will give it back so He can work with it and make it right for you. I was a little upset in the dream and then I remembered God told me already so He must want to fix him up a little bit. So that is what I said in my dream and I felt a sense of peace come over me. When God gives you something you can take that to the bank. He is not man that He should lie. He is not getting a kick out of telling you anything and it not manifesting. You keep talking to Him and He will continue to show you areas in your life that may need deliverance. There are changes that may need to be completed on your behalf. Like I stated in the beginning I have been speaking in tongue. Before I started I heard myself speaking in tongue in the spirit. I was afraid in the beginning. I think that there may be something with this and some of those that are coming in and out of our congregations they may be experiencing some of the spiritual gifts that we are shunning and feeling as if something is wrong with them. They may feel that they are possessed. They may feel that if they keep speaking about it someone is going to call the people with the jackets. There is a pastor here that I think has gone through this. Not only him but a few of our pastors are not equipped with dealing with these spiritual gifts so they turn to drugs, alcohol, and trying to fight it with adultery for lack of knowledge. There are many pastors that I have seen that I know they have gotten to a high level in God and instead of excepting or I will say receiving this gift they feel that they have lost their minds. The main thing that I do see a great deal in our house of worship is these men and some of the women turn to drugs to try to turn off what God has turned on. It is a hurtful thing to see. If you look at some of the people around you that are or were spiritual and see the transformation and you have wondered to yourself what happened to that person that may be what it was that took them over the edge. They didn't have the knowledge of these spiritual gifts because we reject them and don't embrace them. Something to think about isn't it?

Father, I know that I am not a perfect person I thank You that I can speak to You and that you hear me and assist me. I thank You that I am able to speak with You and the enemy doesn't understand what I am saying. I can tell you anything. There is nothing that You don't know and nothing is new to You. I thank You for hearing me when I am sad and when I am happy. I thank You for answering my prayers. Lord, I ask you to help me with speaking in tongue guide me to what I am suppose to say to You. This quality is something that I appreciate. I may not know what I am saying I know that You do thanks for listening. In the name of Jesus Amen

Chapter 5

Dreams and Visions

When we speak of visions what are we truly speaking of? Are visions dreams? Well we will tackle the first question and then move on. Visions are a way that the Father is speaking to us. Sometimes we are able to see visions for ourselves. In my experience the vision is something that is seen while you are awake. For the lack of a better term it is a dream that you are having while you are awake. You are seeing something that is yet to come. You may see something for yourself or something for someone else. You will know the difference if it is for you or another. You have to ask for discernment if you are not able to decipher who the vision is for. There are times that you will have a vision about something for yourself for example and later on that day or maybe even moments from it occurring the vision is manifested in your life. You could have a vision of someone saying boo to you for example and see everything so vividly and then the person comes and says boo. I will admit this is really awesome. I have had so many visions happen to me that have happened maybe the next day. I have spoken things to others that may have taken months or years to manifest in their lives but the key thing is that God is not man that He should lie. He will manifest whatever He has shown and given utterance for You to receive in His time. There may be something that you need to do or a place in your life that you need to be. Not a physical place all the time more spiritually than anything. There are a many a man that someone has spoken the ministry into their lives and they know that at that moment (well they feel) they may not be ready and they may laugh at the vision that the person has had concerning them. The laughter is only that they fail to understand that the word has been spoken into existence this is the time that they should take to start getting themselves ready for their spiritual journey but many of them will continue the path to their demise. What they fail to realize is that God said it and it is done. It will not happen when you are ready for it that is just to get you ready for what God is about to do in your life. The ministry is not for everyone and most of the ministers have to go through to present the word to the non believers. You may be getting ready to speak the word to someone who is going to also be placed in the ministry of God. When you have spoken this word to whomever you are led don't watch their every move. You have done your duty now you just sit back and watch unless you have something else to speak into their spirit. It is an awesome thing to watch the manifestation of our Lord and Savior. Some may feel that they are not ready when the Father is ready for you to shake rattle and roll you are going to do it! Obadiah has one chapter in the Bible. In the beginning of this chapter it starts off by stating "This is the vision that the Sovereign Lord revealed to Obadiah…" The Lord reveals to us in visions and dreams. He not only will give you a vision and a dream but if you are unable to understand what you have seen He will also give you wisdom if you ask for it. There have been times that I have seen something and not understood what it meant for the person or for myself so I may ask God what it means and He reveals it to me either through me or through someone or something around me. There are times that it may not be meant for you to know what He is speaking of. He may just have the message for the person that you are speaking to. This is something that is not turned on and off by us. God will use you when and as He sees fit. You may have the ability today to read everyone around you and then tomorrow you may not see anything. This is something that is not under your control.

You also have to make sure you are living your life in the proper manner and doing the will of God and not your own will. In Joel 2:28 it states that it shall come to pass afterward, that I will pour out my spirit upon all flesh; and your sons and your daughter shall prophesy, your old men shall dream dreams, your young men shall see visions: Our pastors and many others will not except this passage as for our right now time. They will go back to the Old Testament for the "Virtuous Women" in Proverbs 31 and the Psalm 23 to tell you that the Lord is your shepherd. Many members will also delight you with Ecclesiastes 3 telling you that "To everything there is a season, and a time to every purpose under the heaven:" This is the time for us to stand up and be accounted for. This is time for the good fight of faith to be fought by those that know that they know God will fight the battle for them because it is not your fight but the Lords! Hello somebody. .

When I first started I would go to the bathroom at church and pray a little and cry a little and make sure that I was supposed to say what I felt led to say and I would also pray for strength because I knew someone was going to try to attack me. After I would pray I would go out and say what God wanted me to say. I felt led on many occasions to speak to this little girl and tell her that her friends were not her friends and that things were going to happen to her that didn't have to if she would just listen to her mother and the people that really loved her. We went over how love is an action word. Reinforcing to her that her mother was showing her love by taking care of her and the "friends" she was so adamant about being around only wanted what they could get out of her and when that ran out she wasn't going to have that "friend" any longer. I said everything that came to my mind to try to keep her from running away and doing something that I felt was going to change her life forever. She didn't listen to me. I felt bad in the beginning and I prayed. People are around you for a reason. There was someone around me telling me that everything we speak to people is not going to be accepted they will eventually start listening when it is the time for them to listen. I don't know where everyone's journey is going to take them. I am only responsible to speak the things that God is telling me to say and then leave it alone. There will be times that you will have spoken so much to this same person and they still do what is familiar to them. It is time to leave it alone. Don't drop them just don't repeat yourself unless you are led by the Spirit. We are all human and what it takes for you to wake up may take someone else uncountless attempts to free themselves from the demons they are fighting. When you can ask God to show you something or let me receive a message and then the message is not what you wanted so you keep

living and doing as you were, the only way that is
going to be fixed is by an intervention from the
Father above. You are just His vessel to deliver a
message that He has probably sent to this person
Himself. Don't beat yourself up pray yourself
through. What I mean by that is simply we will try
our best to make the person we are speaking to
hear what God is telling them. When they refuse
to change or we don't see the change we cry out
for them, checking on them. After you deliver the
message let it go. You can't make them change
only the Miracle Maker can do that. They have to
want the change. He doesn't do anything that is
wanted by the person. You make things behave in
your path by using your gifts to fight the devil. The
devil wants your mind not your body. Your mind
controls your body. Your mind is helping you see
the visions and the dreams. If your mind is cloudy
then you don't see everything that is coming your
way. You don't see the road blocks or maybe you

see them but your vision is so distorted you were not able to see the vision as it truly was. You may be trying to be a double minded being. That is you are trying to serve God and the enemy because you are not ready to give up those material things that the enemy has let you think belong to you. God wants us to have wealth not money. Money is only a means of negotiation. When you are a part of God all negotiating is over. When you move into your place in God before you get a thought of a want it is manifest in your life no matter what it is. You have gone past the money stage and have stepped into the wealth that God is the only one that can give you. You are not worrying about someone robbing you because this was given to you by God not man and everything that God lets us borrow the only one that can and will take it away is God. You don't have to worry about acquiring fast money because that fast money leaves quickly. You have to walk through the visions and dreams that God has placed around and about you to learn how to keep the money that He is giving you. You have to learn how to appreciate your family so when you are given one you already know that they are not perfect. You may have a family but they may not really be with you. They may not be fighting to assist your path. This is a family journey. The sons of God! God has to take you to another level and then when you are done going through all of those visions and dreams then you have some more that you have to go through and then there is another level to be completed. This is not telling you that because you are having a vision and dream that they are always going to be pleasant because they may not be. Don't be scared just be guided by the Holy Spirit and get the level fixed up so you can move to a new place in God. He is not going to bring you closer to the top level let us say and you have so many lusts and demons going on. He is not trying to have anything corrupt around Him. That is why the devil had to go. He will assist you so that you are able to be in His Presence. To be in His Presence! He is not going to give you more than you can handle it is going to be enough to get that demon out of you. You may be dealing with malice, greed, envy, a liar, a thief, etc. Whatever is not of Him. He already knows who he is going to use for what portion they are going to be needed. You may have a vision about someone around you that may be a hot mess right now and you may see them living their life right in the future and helping out others it will only take you a moment to tell them what God is saying to you. That may be all that is needed in their life. God will chasten us this means that He will correct us by punishment or reproof, or restrain, subdue or chasten a proud spirit or He will rid us of excess things while refining or purifying us. Hebrews 12: 5-7 And ye have forgotten the exhortation which speaketh unto you as unto children, My son, despise not thou the chastening of the Lord, nor faint when thou art rebuked of him: 6 For whom the Lord loveth he chasteneth, and scourgeth every son whom he receiveth. 7 If ye endure chastening, God dealeth with you as with sons; for what son is he whom the father chasteneth not? You are going to have some that will try to have you scared of your gift or may try to have you receive praise for the gifts. God hath not given us the spirit of fear. 2 Timothy 1: 7For God hath not given us the spirit of fear; but of power, and of love, and of a sound mind. Don't allow anyone to praise you for having visions and dreams. John 12: 43For they loved the praise of men more than the praise of God. He is not unrighteous to forget your work and labor of love. Love is a action word. Hebrews 6: 10For God is not unrighteous to forget your work and labour of love, which ye have shewed toward his name, in that ye have ministered to the saints, and do minister. There are so many of our children and the children of others that are going through what you have already had to deal with. Trying to keep this gift quiet and it is not fair! Your child or someone around you has spoken to you and told you that they had a dream about something that is happening to them right now or they are having what we have so ignorantly called de ja vu. There is no such a thing. A vision is a vision is a vision is a vision. No matter how you look at it. Hello somebody.

Father forgive me for the sins that I did that I knew about and the sins that I have done that I didn't know about. I repent of the sins please forgive me. Lord I pray that as I deliver the message given to me by Your precious Holy Spirit that I am able to let go and let you do what You said. Let me be able to release the information from my spirit and move on. I pray that they are delivered from whatever the situation is and that they are walking in the path of Your righteousness. Father I ask that my visions and dreams that are delivered unto me are so vivid that it seems as if I can reach out and touch them. That the information that is delivered to me in visions and dreams are there to not only help others but also available to help my family and I do Your Will. Give me the courage to speak what You have given me to speak whether it is good or bad whether it is to someone that is wanting to see me fail or to the person that is holding my hand here on earth. I love You and I am ready to serve Your purpose in my life. In the name of Jesus I pray Amen.

Chapter 6

Speaking and they don't listen

Boy let me tell you everything that is spoken in that Word is what it is. You can be in the whale of the belly and not even realize it. There are so many instances where I can recall being in the whale and becoming comfortable with living inside this massive belly. Giving up on what God wanted for me and my life. Feeling that I was indeed spit out when I had only been walking around and establishing myself in another portion of the belly of my whale. I have just gotten to the tongue of my whale! I am ready to get out and the way that I am doing this is writing this book. I feel the same way that Jonah felt. I know that this book is not going to be received by many of my peers. But just as Jonah has given up and let go and let God because he is indeed tired of the smell and the same course of walking back and forth in this whale I am also tired and ready to be spit up to see what this word is going to do for many. I know that my part is completed. I know that it is not so much for me as it is for so many to start to come out and experience the awesomeness of God. I know that many of you will read this and be upset that is not my plight it is yours. There are many of you that are going to say it is about time and ask God to help you with what you have been going through and for you this is written. Everyone is not going to except what is being stated in this book I cannot do anything for you. I only can ask God to assist in the deliverance of those that do believe that God is still delivering us in many different ways. The enemy is still in combat with us. The enemy still inhabits the minds and bodies of our people. The enemy is still a dirty fighter so if the enemy is still fighting us using the devices that he has why would God take the tools to fight him away for you to basically fight him in your own fashion. That doesn't make sense to me and it must not make sense to you because you are still reading this book! The enemy came to steal, kill, and destroy. He is after us by any means necessary. This means that he is going to fight you until there is no you to fight. If you are not aware to the tools that are available for you to win this race he is enjoying every grasp that he is getting to do his business. If you are not aware of what gifts you are indeed blessed with you are able to ask God to assist you and He will. It is His will for us to fight the enemy. Everything that is happening now is nothing new. All of this is something that is just reoccurring and it is up to us to take the blinders off and fight the good fight of faith. Some of us are going to continue to take the battle scars and use the greatest tool that we still use and that is prayer. But for those of us that want to assist with the fight for others and we know that we are able to speak with God and fight the battle with the spiritual gifts that are indeed there. They are spoken of in the word so that we know not to be afraid. The enemy is not going to warn you with a vision or a dream that he is going to attack or show you that yes tomorrow you will smile, or even give you the ability to see the danger that he is placing in the path of another. No he is not going to help you. He is strictly there to hurt you to kill you period. There are no if or ands about this. He wants you to deny the gifts of God. I don't know about where you worship I only know that where I worship there are certain scriptures that are not discussed and as they are discussed by the congregation there is a sense of defiance so our pastor gets in defense mode and attacks us. I know that this is only being done because he doesn't know or understand what is being asked nor what these gifts truly consist of. If he was able to truly understanding the scripture that we are speaking to God and that we are able to prophesy he would try

to see what gifts were where in our congregation.
It is time for our pastors and/or the congregation
to come together collectively and fight the enemy.
If we get out of the belly and get out of the fear
and the anger of the whole they are not going to
listen and not worry about they and just do the
Will of God. God is fighting for us we just have to
relinquish the throne and let Him fight our battle.
When we do that and really try to understand the
place God has for us here on earth we will come
to the knowledge that He always wins His battle.
When you read the word you will see that in the
end we win. I am on the winning team. I know
that there are going to be many in denial and they
are going to bash me and say evil things about me.
My flesh isn't going to heaven or hell and man
doesn't have either to place me in. My Father told
me to do something and I am doing it. There are
many of you trying to find your place and trying to
get out of your belly. I tell you

that you just hold on to the unchanging hand of God and don't let go no matter what the circumstances are and He will see you through. No good thing will be held back from you. As I write this book while waiting to be vomited out of my whale I am homeless as you would not believe. When I say homeless we are staying in a hotel there are five of us myself and my children. To see the manifestation of the Glory of God in our lives is so awesome. I have not been wanting for anything. Before a need even truly is examined by me God has already worked it out. This is because I have let go of the mentality of the whale and Mr. Jonah. I knew that this book was to be written and I have written along with this one a few books. I kept telling everyone around me that I know God has me without a home and without a job because He wants me to write. So I would write and write and don't let me fool you I knew that this is the one that He wanted me to write.

But I was so comfortable in the belly of my whale. We have been so blessed with having every need met. I still wasn't ready to feel uncomfortable because I knew just like Jonah that this word was not going to be taken in the manner that I wanted it taken. The way that I know that I perceive it and I was also worried about what everyone that I loved (I didn't say that loved me) would say because we "don't believe in that". I didn't want to be taken out of my comfort zone. Hello somebody. I didn't want my family to look at me in a different manner. I didn't want to be embarrassed. It was all about me. God showed me that it is not about them nor is it about you it is about His Will. I had to learn how to depend on Him because through everything that I have gone through my God has gotten me through it all. I have had my leg broken and been knocked unconscious and told that I would never walk again. But God. I have been without a job for so long. But God. I have been talked about and false accused. But God. I can go on and on and on and I am sure that a lot of you have also had the experience of going through. I am here to tell you that you are not going through just to have a notch on your belt. God is doing something with you. It is time for us to get out of the belly of our whales and time for us to fight the good fight. I am tired of the enemy fighting dirty and we are all dumbfounded because we don't want anyone besides some of our friends and family knowing what God has blessed us with. You do realize that this is a blessing. I don't know why you have it I just know that it is there and God is doing wonders and He is awesome. There are many instances where a prophet or prophetess has spoken to masses of individuals and their words have not been taken seriously. This is especially evident when it is something that either the prophet is refusing to inform you or you don't like the information that has been given to you. We really don't like it when the mate we have chosen isn't the person we are supposed to be with. We will find every excuse in the world to keep them around even if they are being pushed from our lives. Many individuals that are spoken of in the Bible had to come from a place of disgrace and then get into the "Glory of God' to be set out so that people dealing with the same issues or with issues greater or less than theirs so that all of us can see some of these people and places that they had to come from in our lives. We would let the enemy stay on attack if there weren't examples of people being a hit man as Paul who was and then transformed into a Christian. Isaac who was a daydreamer transformed into a Christian. Jacob who manipulated many turned into a Christian. Joseph was abused and rejected by his family and sold into slavery and then went to jail so he was an ex con and became second in control of the whole kingdom. These stories give us hope and the knowledge to know that if they can do it I can to. There is nothing new under the sun. Moses had a stuttering problem and he was able to lead his nation to a great victory. Sampson was a womanizer and Rahab was a prostitute and they were able to worship God and they made changes that no one else had the authority to do. You are the captain of your own fate. They said Timothy was too young and he was able to go and preach the word of God by the magnificent manifestation of Jesus Christ. Jonah was prejudice and God was able to show him that he wasn't right using the anger that he had for the people he was supposed to speak to and a plant to show him that He was still in control and He is the God of second chance. Esther was adopted by a whole nation and yet through her blood line the Word became flesh and dwelt among us. She didn't know what she was doing it just felt right to her. You don't know who you are birthing and who they will birth into this world. Your every move affects your whole bloodline. Everything that you do has an effect on those that you may never meet. The decisions you make to save a little, to mean something and leave an imprint on your family and the world, and your decision to place down all of the things that you are doing that you know is not right in the sight of God will affect everyone around you and after you. If you instill hate in your seed that is all they will know until someone comes up out of your seed and shows something different. If you show them the love of God and how to handle issues that may not feel good but rather get the lesson to be learned and teach it to your children and to others around you this is setting something great in motion. Naomi didn't let the bitterness that she was feeling from stopping the lesson that she was teaching to Ruth. The lesson with their relationship was the elder women teaching the younger women. Esther had no idea when she was taken and adopted by the palace that she would become a queen and deliver her people from being slaughtered. She had fear and she dealt with it in prayer and she had others pray and fast with her for their deliverance for her safety. Where three or four of you come together He will be there. Job had to go through bankruptcy and he knew that he was not in defiance with God and he knew that God was going to deliver him out of his situation even if it was through death. Through his trial he was given double for his trouble. Don't get mad get on your knees as you are going through you don't have to know why or for what just ask for strength and that you are led down the path of righteousness and the His Glory is manifested in your situation and in your life. God has birthed all of them out of their situations and if He can take them from dramatic situations and pasts He can do the same for you. We had some believers back then. They didn't have the television, phone, internet, or any fast means of communication as we do. They knew that God was capable. We have all of this when someone calls us with a problem and then we see the victory manifest in their lives. We go through our situations we don't have the courage to know that God is going to do what He said He was going to do. They had faith back then. Where are our faith warriors today?

Father, give me strength and courage to know that you are going to do everything that You stated in my life and in the lives of the believers. Teach me how to become stronger and not to worry or waiver from the disappointment and disbelief of my neighbor. Let me search Your word on a daily basis. Wake me up and give me revelations and visions so that I am aware of my surroundings. Teach me how to discern the people and places that are around me. Give me the courage that Esther had when she went before the king as she didn't realize her fate she trusted that You were going to deliver her out of the hands of death and You did Father. Deliver me from my fears. Teach me how to teach my children the strength and courage of Your understanding and not our own. Help me to not care what others say discouraging about me You are my Provider. I am an joint heir according to the promise I am not disqualified to do Your Will. In the name of Jesus.

Amen

Chapter 7

Prophesying

While you are giving a vision and the utterance of the vision sometimes you are also given prophesy for someone or maybe even yourself. The information that is needed by everyone the information is reaching out to. There will be times in the beginning that you may not know who the information the Holy Spirit is giving belongs to but after the information is delivered to you and you analyze and ask who it is for you will be given all the information. Look at Numbers 11:29 And Moses said unto him, Enviest thou for my sake? Would God that all the LORD'S people were prophets, and that the LORD would put his spirit upon them! There are so many instances in the Word that clearly tell us that having the spiritual gifts is here today and it has not gone. These scriptures are in the Old and New Testament. I have grown to the realization that most things that are spoken in the Old Testament are overlooked because it is in the Old Testament and much of the Old is tied into the New but if it is something that is not understood by our brethren for whatever reason it is said it is muted or gone. Don't let the devil steal your joy. It is joyful to be able to speak to your children or even to anyone in general and tell them something that the Holy Spirit has shared with you. Luke 1:67And his father Zacharias was filled with the Holy Ghost, and prophesied. It may not come to manifestation right then and there it will come into manifestation in His time not yours. It is great to have those same people come back to you and tell you" thanks" or "you were correct I should have listened." It is time for this activation to happen in the Church of Christ. 1 Peter 4:11If any man speak, let him speak as the oracles of God; if any man minister, let him do it as of the ability which

God giveth: that God in all things may be glorified through Jesus Christ, to whom be praise and dominion forever and ever. Amen. When you speak you need to remove all the fear that will try to creep into your spirit to tell you not to do this and call you all kind of crazy. That is the devil. Don't listen. The Spirit didn't give you the information just to give it to you. Don't hold back what God has given you through His precious Holy Spirit. 2 Samuel 23:2 The Spirit of the LORD spake by me, and his word was in my tongue. It is time for us to place the spirit of fear and put on the armor of God. Luke 1:37 For with God nothing shall be impossible. God wants the prophetic ministry to be activated where you are and where I am. You are not alone this is a journey that is going to evoke many emotions because it is indeed something new and something that has been said we are not supposed to do in service. They are going to tell you that next we are going to try to have the instruments coming in. In the word it doesn't say that all instruments are not supposed to be in our service it gives us the ones that we are able to sing hymns to but I don't see our ministers trying to get that together because of fear. We sound nice on Sundays don't get me wrong just giving you something to help you with the fight! We are moving the Church out of denial. Joel 2:28And it shall come to pass afterward, that I will pour out my spirit upon all flesh; and your sons and your daughters shall prophesy, your old men shall dream dreams, your young men shall see visions: I have been seeing and prophesying to myself and to close friends and family not all but some. What is so amazing is my grandfather had a dream. My van was stolen while I was sleeping and while I was asleep the Spirit let me see the person steal it. While he was stealing the van he looked up at my window and then he drove off. This all was for my walk of faith. When I woke up and saw my van was gone all I could do was laugh and praise God. When I called and told my grandmother she was upset and I told her not to worry God was going to handle the whole situation. My grandfather was just as calm as I was and he also knew who had stolen my van. He was also shown that it would return a week later. It was stolen on a Sunday and was found on the following Sunday. The Holy Spirit showed my grandfather the person that had stolen my van and the Sunday that it was returned he told me that he had a dream that night that my van was going to be spotted that day. He walked into his office at church and no sooner than he and I sat down he called me into his office and told me that someone spotted my van and the person that had stolen it was pushing it with someone else. As I have stated I was never worried. I know that God is doing something. You have to look to the hills from whence cometh your help. You have to really look to see the victory. We all are able to not only have spiritual gifts but use them for the glory of God. We will say something about de ja vu when things are happening that we have seen some place before. I don't know who de ja vu is. I do know that he didn't send anyone here to die for me nor did he let the Holy Spirit be poured out on me. This de ja vu fellow needs to show himself to me and to you as well. We need to step into the light and get out of stepping into the dark side. When we deny what God is doing in our lives we are denying Him. I know I have said that before it is the truth. Job 32: 8But there is a spirit in man: and the inspiration of the Almighty giveth them understanding. If there is something that you do not understand ask Him He is the only one that has the right answer. If you don't believe what I am telling you about any of what I have said and the things that are yet to come ask Him. Don't take my word or any man's word for anything that is going on in your life ask the one that created you and see what He comes back with. Just be ready to accept the answer. Your eyes are being opened to the true righteousness and the greatest glory in this world and that is a intimate relationship with God. It is time for you to place the bottle of milk that you have been using to get your feeding and grab that steak cooked just the way you like it. Come closer to His glory. You won't return null and void. This is the fight for the fittest the ones that have endurance and the courage to be different. We are different because we see what God is saying very loudly. While you are going through all of the awesomeness of God there are going to be so many great occurrences that no one is going to be able to explain to you because it was your time with the King. Get ready to go to the higher place in God that you have been asking for. Watch what you are uttering out of your mouth. Watch every move grab a hold of the hand of God and don't let go. You may have smoked cigarettes before, drank liquor by the gallon, cursed like Peter, or persecute everyone around you as Saul did before he was Paul; today is the day you make your change. If you give all of this to Him and let it go and let Him make you over you will be so amazed when you see the outcome of the new you. The person that was already there just waiting for something to spark your light. You may now consider yourself lit. 2 Thessalonians 2:15-17 15Therefore, brethren, stand fast, and hold the traditions which ye have been taught, whether by word, or our epistle. 16Now our Lord Jesus Christ himself, and God, even our Father, which hath loved us, and hath given us everlasting consolation and good hope through grace, 17Comfort your hearts, and stablish you in every good word and work. And believe like you have never believed in your life that God is doing this not you or anyone else. Pray for direction with everything you do. This is right and if you were not supposed to help out this then you would not be reading this. Don't doubt yourself at all. Luke 1:45And blessed is she that believed: for there shall be a performance of those things which were told her from the Lord. Watch God bless you.

Father, throughout the word there has been a prophet available to kings for the use of the kingdom. The kingdom has placed many great men and women at the fore front and some yet to come for Your Will they are in need of direction that is give by prophetic intervention. Father, let those individuals that are in need of direction to assist in Your Kingdom be made aware of the prophetic individuals that are in our midst. Not the false prophet Father, but the ones that are placed by You. Let the individuals that are in need of direction when they are approached by those that are speaking prophet have the courage and the knowledge to ask these prophetic speakers who sent them and if they say God they ask what God? Let only prophets that are in Your Will be aligned to those that are in need and let them be around individuals that have the direction of what You have in store for our great nation. We are not able to be sufficient in anything God without Your direction. We have gotten ourselves in a jam and only You are able to take us through this battle and align us with the victory through Jesus Christ and this is only to be done if we submit ourselves. I am submitting that I need you God. Please help me to help those that You direct me to. Let Your Love shine through my vessel. In the mighty name of Jesus I pray. Amen.

Chapter 8

What Others Think

While you are going through this journey for the Lord you are going to be shot down and feeling overwhelmed. You are going to have so many different emotions that you may not have felt in a while. You are going to want to give up, become depressed, doubting your gifts, etc. This is the enemy attacking you to make you desire to give up. Your family, friends, and members of the church or going to try everything to assist you in giving up on these gifts. The enemy is going to attack you with everything and with everyone that you are not even thinking about. They don't mean to do it and they may not know what they are doing. You just have to stay praying and fasting for strength to continue your path. When you allow them to get to you this is the enemy just trying to have his way in your life. The best way for the devil to attack you is by using the things that are close to you. What are the things close to you? You have to ask yourself what or who you are afraid of finding out about the gifts that you have. Strategies just as if you are fighting a war as you look at it and get the wisdom and knowledge you will see that this is indeed a war. When you don't let go of your family and friends and you are expecting their respect you will fall out of your place with God because you have not let go and let God. 1 Corinthians 14:1-5 1Follow after charity, and desire spiritual gifts, but rather that ye may prophesy. 2For he that speaketh in an unknown tongue speaketh not unto men, but unto God: for no man understandeth him; howbeit in the spirit he speaketh mysteries. 3But he that prophesieth speaketh unto men to edification, and exhortation, and comfort. 4He that speaketh in an unknown tongue edifieth himself; but he that prophesieth edifieth the church. 5I would that ye all spake with tongues but rather that ye prophesied: for greater is he that prophesieth than he that speaketh with tongues, except he interpret, that the church may receive edifying. Don't allow the tragedies that will start coming around and about you to make you feel that you are on the wrong path. I assure you that you are on the proper journey. Your family and friends at church are going to do everything in their power to get you to act like them. But you have seen and feel the destiny that was just waiting for you to awaken. There is a need for us to search out our spiritual gifts and while searching God is going to give each person the role that they must play in His plan for His glory. Please align yourself so everything that is to be done is done. There is a fight that is going on all over our nation that needs to be addressed and we need to aid in the efforts that so many have already treaded the path to help deliver you from the wilderness. It is now time for us to complete what has already been started.

Nothing that is happening now has taken long for the delivery it is all done in decent order. We as a nation have done something that was thought to never of happened but because we believed in change and we knew that God was in control we prayed for change and received it. It happened in a decent order. 1 Corinthians 14:39-40 Wherefore, brethren, covet to prophesy, and forbid not to speak with tongues. 40Let all things be done decently and in order. This is the time for the order to begin. Many of His warriors are being strategically placed for this fight. There is a need for our leadership to understand and lead us into the Will of God but as we know when they are not ready He will pull out ordinary and make them extraordinary. Some of the leadership is going to stand up and fight for this cause and then there will be some that will fight for it but want a profit from it. Be careful. Find a group of Christians that are opening up their spiritual eye and you all try to pray and learn together. Pray for a strong leader to submerge and walk you into what thus says the Lord. Your faith and confidence is going to stir up so strongly. You are going to amaze yourself. Ask and receive what is ready to be given to you only after you ask for it. Research the gifts that are available to you as a Christian and ask for them. Ask for direction to use the gifts. Matthew 7:7-11 7Ask, and it shall be given you; seek, and ye shall find; knock, and it shall be opened unto you: 8For every one that asketh receiveth; and he that seeketh findeth; and to him that knocketh it shall be opened. 9Or what man is there of you, whom if his son ask bread, will he give him a stone? 10Or if he ask a fish, will he give him a serpent? 11If ye then, being evil, know how to give good gifts unto your children, how much more shall your Father which is in heaven give good things to them that ask him? When you ask and your heart is pure and it is your desire to serve God then there is nothing that He will keep from you. Titus 1:15Unto the pure all things are pure: but unto them that are defiled and unbelieving is nothing pure; but even their mind and conscience is defiled. 16They profess that they know God; but in works they deny him, being abominable, and disobedient, and unto every good work reprobate. Stop denying what God can do. Don't deny what He is doing in your life. Turn away from the sins that you know about and ask for help with the sins that you don't know about. None of us are perfect and He knows that. Don't let yourself stay on the wheel to nowhere telling yourself that you are going to be right later be right now. Don't let the denials that others around you are condemning themselves to become latched onto what God is trying to do for you in your life. Your family and friends are going to attack you with everything that they have. Some of them don't know what they are doing and some of them do. Whether they know or not if you have to stay away from them for a while to receive your spiritual gifts then that is what you do. When it is time to meet Him they can't say "wait that didn't happen because of us." They can't vouch for you or anyone else. In the end we all have to stand before Him on our own and give an account to everything that we have done and the things that we didn't do. You are going to be in church services and receive a word from God! What are you going to do with it? Please don't hold it in speak it to whomever He is giving it for. Pray for them before you deliver it to them. Pray that they receive the message and understand what God is saying to them. Pray that you have the confidence to deliver the message the way that God wants it delivered and that you are speaking to the correct person. Romans 12: 6Having then gifts differing according to the grace that is given to us, whether prophecy, let us prophesy according to the proportion of faith; There are some that are going to come to you for a word every time they see you. Many will even call your phone off the hook. I had to turn my phone off. A lot of the things that I had to speak to many family members they were very upset about them. I had to make sure that I was supposed to tell them and when I knew that it was for me to speak it I spoke it. The medicine for most of them didn't taste too good. Many probably thought I was just saying something to get back for all the evil I felt coming from them. My one aunt I would see her in the spirit praying when she was younger and I told her that God wanted her to pray more. She got so mad about that prayer. It is not for you to receive the messages for these people they have to receive it and do what thus says the Lord. You have done your part after you tell them what the Spirit led you to say. When God tells you to leave it alone and for so many of them He will tell you to leave it alone because they will ask you the same questions and receive the same answers or for many they feel that they can fool God. Then you will have those that will either tell you that you are getting the information from someone else or that you don't know what you are talking about. You need only deliver the message and watch God in those friends and families lives. 2 Timothy 4:3For the time will come when they will not endure sound doctrine; but after their own lusts shall they heap to themselves teachers, having itching ears; It is time for you to place on your big girl/boy underwear and only care about what the one that can destroy both your body and your soul has to say. I know that most of our parents have spoken to us and have told us that it doesn't matter what anyone has to say about you it is how you feel about yourself. It is time for you to work on your self esteem. We need to stop worrying about the naysayers. There has always been someone saying something about you right or wrong? Each and every time someone has some ill begotten things to say to or about you there is no way that you are going to be able to correct everything they are feeling about you. You may be able to speak something that they didn't know about you which is still not going to change how that person perceives you. Jeremiah 1: 10See, I have this day set thee over the nations and over the kingdoms, to root out, and to pull down, and to destroy, and to throw down, to build, and to plant. When you take on what God has for you and understand your gifts as you settle the enemy is going to place people in your path that will make you second guess yourself. You have to pray for what you need and receive it and let it go. These people are eventually going to be seen as what they are and dealt with until then you are going to have to stand your ground and be a hard fighting soldier. You are not mistaken you have gifts. The weapons that you are able to use to pull down these strong holds and these weapons are your spiritual gifts. Learn how to use them. 2 Corinthians 10: 4(For the weapons of our warfare are not carnal, but mighty through God to the pulling down of strong holds;). The spiritual gifts that you have are going to make so many people upset and bring about many envious individuals. They will attempt to tear down your character and make you feel every part of a traitor. Remember they don't hold the key to your salvation. Job 18:14His confidence shall be rooted out of his tabernacle, and it shall bring him to the king of terrors. When you allow Him to assist you with the spiritual gifts and stop refusing to let go of what you feel He is able to do then the house of the Lord shall flourish in His courts. Psalm 92:13Those that be planted in the house of the LORD shall flourish in the courts of our God. The Word gives us words for those who may go around shaming you. Let the enemy be ashamed and sore vexed. Let them turn and be ashamed and suddenly as in Psalm 6: 10Let all mine enemies be ashamed and sore vexed: let them return and be ashamed suddenly. Fight for a change in your spirit so you don't care what anyone around you has to say about you. There is no fear in God. There is no misinformation in God. The people that are speaking ill of you love you being in hardship and not understanding what God has for you. Many of the people that are around you don't want prosperity to come knocking at your door. Misery loves company. There are those that around you everyday smiling in your face and discrediting you behind your back they are wolves in sheep clothing. The enemy will use these people to keep you from performing the great things that God has for you to do for His kingdom. You are not ready for it because you are worried about these people that you feel love you and are looking out for your best interest. I don't know any of them that will have their life taken so you are able to flourish and repent for anything for that matter. Think about what Jesus has done for you. There are days that there was no way anything was going to happen on any side of the coin. Jesus set you free. Just think if He thought about what all those people were saying about Him. They were looking at where He came from. Meaning who His parents were and the lineage that came with that. They were looking at where He was from as a province. They looked at so many different factors that were telling them socially that this Man is not in a place to tell me anything. But Jesus didn't listen to them He perceived because He knew who he was and it didn't matter if they accepted Him or not you have to tell yourself that I can do this and I am somebody. If He would have let them get to Him where would we be? When He was not accepted He shook that dust from His feet and He left. It is time to shack it and leave. You don't have to tell them that you are done with them. Your actions speak louder. If it is in the Will of God they will be okay and that relationship will be mended but if you continue to try to fix this and they continue to speak to your spirit and tear what God has built up you will start believing as they believe that you are nothing!

God use me for Your Will and guide me through the traps that have been set out for a distraction to keep me from helping the person that is need of You in their lives. Let me not lean on my own understanding nor what everyone else perceives me to be only what You have said and filled in me before I knew who I was. Fill me with Your Holy Spirit to guide me. I have done it my way now I am trying it Your way. I love You God. I love You Jesus. Amen

Chapter 9

Getting your armor together for the fight

When He stated that the battle is not yours it's the Lord's that really means something. There is nothing that anyone can say or do to you. God has you covered. If it was not noticed when they were imprisoned and they began to sing and pray then the shackles were loosened and the gates of the jail came open. Hello somebody. Let us take a trip back even further. Cain killed Abel and his spirit cried out to God and He heard him. You can do things and think you will get away but God….but God knows it all. He already knows what we are going to do before we do it. We don't know. He can tell us (and He has through His Word) every step we are going to make and when we are going to get it right our flesh will take over and doubt Him. He knows what He is doing. The world can persecute you as long as you have the Master the knowing all and seeing all on your side that is all you need. You believe in your deliverance and bam there it is. It is not easy and it is not given to the one that gets to the end first it is given to the one that endures to the end. When you endure that is telling everyone something. What you may ask is it telling? It is telling everyone that you went through something. It wasn't just handed down to you. You didn't inherit your place. You had to work for this place. You had to go through something to get to this place. We have to go through to get the victory. When we get done there is a battle of all battles and it is needed to be known by you that you are able to fight and you are not scared of anything that is coming your way. God is on your side. Jesus is real. You are coming through with the victory. It is a great thing to know that no matter what is said or done in the end if you hold on and don't let go God is going to see you through whatever the situation you are facing.

There are going to be times that you are going to place your head in your lap and cry like a baby some of you will let the Comforter fill you with His comfort some of you will try to resolve your own issue and have to go through all over again. Yes, you have to go through. When you let the Comforter take the front seat and guide you through in the path of His righteousness then you will realize that you know someone. You do realize that you know someone? He is the Alpha and Omega that means something. To know that I have the creator of Heaven and Earth on my side means that there is nothing that anyone can say or do that will make me change the way I feel about Him. I know that when it is all said and done He loves me even more than I love myself. He loves me more than my mother, father, sister, children, etc. He loves me and the only thing He wants me to do is to follow His instructions and not yours. He wants me to live my life right and help save the lost sheep. He wants me to ask and receive knowledge and wisdom. He wants me to have faith beyond even my own understanding. I have the armor in His Word. There is safety in His arms. His arms are His Word. The Word became flesh and dwelt among us. His Word saved my life. In John's gospel it states that In the beginning was the Word, and the Word was with God, and the Word was God. All things are made by him; and without Him was not anything made that was made. In Him was life; and the life was the light of men. His safety is around and about me. I don't have to see Him or smell Him to know that He is. I feel His presence in my life every day. When I feel like I can't make it I pray for strength and He gives it to me. I pray for protection and that His angels are encamped around and about me and I know that He hears me and that because I am living my life for Him and doing His Will He keeps us safe. Matthew 11:28-30 Come unto me, all ye that labour and are heavy laden, and I will give you rest. Take my yoke upon you, and learn of me; I am meek and lowly in heart: and ye shall find rest unto your souls. For my yoke is easy, and my burden is light. God is telling us to fight and He has our back. Psalm 130:6My soul waiteth for the Lord more than they that watch for the morning: I say, more than they that watch for the morning. Psalm 27:14 **Wait** on the **LORD**: be of good courage, and he shall strengthen thine heart: **wait**, I say, on the **LORD**. The Lord will fight the battle when you are ready to let Him. It is time for the members of the Church of Christ to speak and not to hold our tongues any longer. It is time for us to speak up. Search the word for yourself and get the answers that are needed. Isaiah 62:6I have set watchmen upon thy walls, O Jerusalem, which shall never hold their peace day nor night: ye that make mention of the LORD, keep not silence. Believe beyond where you are in your life right now. God wants to use all of us but we have to submit to His Will. You have to deny your flesh. Look forward and tell those that don't know that whatever happened in your past stays in your past. God has forgiven you and you have moved forward that has made you who you are today. Miracles are happening now through His believers there is a yoke that is going to be broken off of the minds of the believers. The next move of God is coming from the pew and not the pulpit. The pulpit has the responsibility of teaching the saints and the saints are to go out into the world preaching, demonstrating, and manifesting the gospel. It is the responsibility of the church to make the devil behave. The Protocol Son wasn't himself for some time but when he came to himself he was in the world. This person had to hit rock bottom and then be lifted up by his father. His father showed him love. He didn't tell him I told you so. He accepted him back into his home with open arms and gave him a celebration. There are times that we think we have gone out into the world and we feel that we have to get right to come back to God I am here to tell you that it is not so. God wants you to come home. He knew that you were going to make a mistake He sent His only Begotten Son to come here just for when we fall. You fell now get back up. You went to the bottom of nothingness and wallowed with the worst of the worst and you didn't eat the best that He was there waiting for you to eat. He knows that through all that you have gone through you are now ready to help the rest of those that are looking and thinking it looks like fun at the bars, going to parties, taking drugs, drinking and smoking. You are able to do that because you lived it. It is now time for you to come back home. Don't let the enemy tell you that He doesn't want you He does. He knows that you let your flesh take over now let Him get you back into His Will. All you have to do is speak to Him ask for forgiveness and walk right and when the naysayers come and bother you the blood of Jesus is your tool. There are no perfect people. Get back into your position and fight this fight. You were fighting to stay away when you would get up and want to go to church in the spirit and then your flesh told you not to go you let that fight keep you in bed. Now let the fight be the good fight of faith. God is ready for you to come home and commune with Him and we miss you to!

Father, we thank You for answering our prayers and bringing the lost home and we ask that you help us to keep them home. God we know that there is not a perfect person. Help those that don't understanding that to come to that understanding. We need you to help us with our building blocks in our churches. We need your understanding and wisdom in our lives. Guide me and help me to keep my hand in Your Unchanging Hand. Give me the courage I need to be still when they are persecuting me and give it to

You. Guide my mouth to only speak things that are of Your Word. Don't let me fall into the malice and misfortune that they are speaking let that be the downfall of my enemy. Let me continue to show You that I understand my repentance I gave it to You and You have forgiven me. You are worthy to be worshipped and praised. You are always glorified you have done so much for me. I praise you in worship in praise always. In the mighty name of Jesus. Amen.

Chapter 10

Journey

The journey you are on has not just started this is just going to assist you in your preparation for longevity. Wow. Acts 2:17-21 17And it shall come to pass in the last days, saith God, I will pour out of my Spirit upon all flesh: and your sons and your daughters shall prophesy, and your young men shall see visions, and your old men shall dream dreams: 18And on my servants and on my handmaidens I will pour out in those days of my Spirit; and they shall prophesy: 19And I will shew wonders in heaven above, and signs in the earth beneath; blood, and fire, and vapour of smoke: 20The sun shall be turned into darkness, and the moon into blood, before the great and notable day of the Lord come: 21And it shall come to pass, that whosoever shall call on the name of the Lord shall be saved. We are about to see many signs in our churches are you ready for your journey. There were so many miracles that were performed for our direction our instruction in the Word. The journey is not for the ones that are fearful. It will be nice for you to assist in the paving of the way. Pray to be delivered from what you are scared of. I hope by this point that fear is gone. The Church of Christ is missing members because most of these members or even some visitors know what God has given them and they know how to use this spiritual gift when they attend our services they are beaten down and told that what they are feeling is misunderstanding. They have not been misunderstood we have just denied what great things God is doing and has done. The journey has begun. The battle is not given to the one that got there before you it is given to the one that endures to the end. When God closes a door don't stand there crying keep on pressing toward what God has for you. You are a peacemaker. You are

helping your congregation move out of denial.
Matthew 5:9Blessed are the peacemakers: for they
shall be called the children of God.

Your steps are ordered by the Lord no matter your
feelings of insecurity you are not a grasshopper.
David thought he was small but he was only small
in his own mind he was a giant in the eyes of God.
1 Samuel 17 he was able to conquer this giant
because he placed his fear on the back burner. He
believed in himself and it didn't matter that
everyone else had fear he had the courage that you
are going to have to muster up and get this done.
You are going to have to look the giant of fear in
the eye and conquer it. You are going to have to
face the fear of what everyone around you is going
to say. You have to know that you are not going to
be defeated that all is right in your land. It is.
Watch yourself be blessed because you are
stepping out on faith. When the people that are in
the Bible woke up they didn't know that they were

going to perform something great for the glory of God. When Samuel was left at the temple after being weaned from his mother she never explained to him that he was going to do something special. Hannah hadn't realized the effect that her son was going to have on the lives of those around him. Read 1 Samuel. This journey is going to show you that you are a joint heir with Christ and that you have the victory through Christ. Romans 8:17And if children, then heirs; heirs of God, and joint-heirs with Christ; if so be that we suffer with him, that we may be also glorified together. 1 Corinthians 15:57But thanks be to God, which giveth us the victory through our Lord Jesus Christ. After reading the word on a daily basis as we are to search the scriptures the journey will open up the direction in which you are traveling. God will let you see visions of the journey that you are taking. Give thanks to God for the depth of His scriptures and how they are helping. When you are being attacked on this journey by your enemy the word says your enemies fall. Psalm 63: 10They shall fall by the sword: they shall be a portion for foxes. Let God's hand establish you and let His arm strengthen you as you walk in to His Glory. Psalm 89:21With whom my hand shall be established: mine arm also shall strengthen him. Surround yourself with songs of deliverance Psalm 32:7. When you need to be delivered from sexual sin that you have been involved with in the past, including fornication, masturbation, pornography, perversion, fantasy, adultery, drunkenness, etc. and present your body to the Lord as a living sacrifice Romans 12: 1I beseech you therefore, brethren, by the mercies of God, that ye present your bodies a living sacrifice, holy, acceptable unto God, which is your reasonable service. God speaks to us and tells us in His word that we are members of Christ and He will not let us be the members of harlot. When you are fighting a battle things will get a little pushy from the side of the enemy he will place all the impurities that you may have already fought and received the victory back in your life. You have to remember that we are fighting with a dirty fighter the journey is yours but you have to fight. 1 Corinthians 6:15Know ye not that your bodies are the members of Christ? shall I then take the members of Christ, and make them the members of an harlot? God forbid. While you are on the journey please research the Bible. Study the Word so when issues come up you can cry out and tell God in Your word Father, sanctify me through Your Word of truth John 17: 17Sanctify them through thy truth: thy word is truth. Let me be one with my brothers and sisters that the world might believe I have been sent as in John 17: 21That they all may be one; as thou, Father, art in me, and I in thee, that they also may be one in us: that the world may believe that thou hast sent me. Ask God to let you be counted worthy of your calling and fulfill all the good pleasure of His goodness and the work of faith with power as in 2 Thessalonians 1: 11Wherefore also we pray always for you, that our God would count you worthy of this calling, and fulfill all the good pleasure of his goodness, and the work of faith with power: Through your journey don't forget that you are able to bind and loose in heaven and earth. Bind the principalities, powers, rulers of the darkness of this world and spiritual wickedness in high places as in Ephesians 6:12For we wrestle not against flesh and blood, but against principalities, against powers, against the rulers of the darkness of this world, against spiritual wickedness in high places. Loose your neck from all bands as in Isaiah 52:2Shake thyself from the dust; arise, and sit down, O Jerusalem: loose thyself from the bands of thy neck, O captive daughter of Zion. Loose your finances from every spirit of poverty, debt, and lack. God wants us to have wealth not money.

Money is only a means of negotiation. Negotiation is over when you are a part of God. Jesus speaks this in Matthew when speaking to the devil tell him that he is not going to get your mind trying to have you negotiate about something that doesn't belong to him. The devil knows that when he gets your mind he has you. Your mind controls your whole body. That is why he uses things like drugs and alcohol to keep your mind in utter distress and depending on the cloudiness that you have allowed to become dependent. When you let God take control through His precious Holy Spirit everything that you felt impossible starts to become possible. You get the victory. It is already yours. The prize is yours and you then know that you can win. Your head will be held up high and your faith will be so strong. You ever noticed the ones that do come out of whatever addictions they may have suffered from are the ones that are leading and speaking and at the head of many organizations or kingdoms if you will. The enemy knew what he was going to have to fight against with that person on the righteous side. So he will use whatever addiction you have to control you. When you are in an addiction you try to please and get praise from those that are around more than doing what is correct. You don't care who you hurt or whose love you throw away. In 1 John 12: 43For they loved the praise of men more than the praise of God. When you know better you do better. Everything that we allowed to be stolen by the devil has already been redeemed when you align back through Christ and the great gift of repentance. God is restoring your mind to walk into the manifestation that is yours. Wealth of the wicked is laid up for the righteous to come so God can teach you how to think and how to acquire and establish your wealth. We are told in His word in 2: Chronicles 7:14 If my people, which are called by my name, shall humble themselves, and pray, and seek my face, and turn from their wicked ways; then will I hear from heaven, and will forgive their sin, and will heal their land. God wants to use you but just like any opportunity Matthew 22: 14For many are called, but few are chosen. Don't become frustrated. The frustration comes in when we set a level for what God can do for us. When you let others set the level of where you are in God.

Father, I ask You for prophetic insight and to be able to have words spoken that are of Your Will and not mine to be granted and manifested into my life. Transform my life and the lives of those that I have spoken or will speak to. You are bringing us into a proper plan and position. The anointing will come out in each individual as You grant accordingly. The Holy Spirit will carry the anointing to the one that is making the demand to the one that is hungry to be filled. Fill me right now please Father. Anoint me with fresh oil on my head right now. In the mighty and precious name of my Lord and Savior Jesus Christ.

Amen

Chapter 11

Time to Fight

Now it is time for us to fight the good fight of faith. I have the faith that you will be successful with the fight that has been stirred up in your soul. God knows what He is doing. He knows all. I want the One that knows all to help me in all. I have been going through this life as many of you have in drive. I have relinquished the driver's seat to the best driver in the universe. I have placed my life on cruise control. I just sit back and let God do what needs to be done. I don't mean that I am not doing anything. My works are not dead. I know that everything going on about and around me is going to be handled by Him. I don't worry about what man has to say or what he does. I just look and keep it moving. Before I am in bed I pray and let go and let God. When you know God it is something awesome. I am fighting this fight because I know that this is God's Will for my life to be out here fighting this battle and helping others to take off the blindfolds and fight. When the enemy is revealed in your life then you just look at how God has brought you out of so much. He has been fighting for you all this time and now it is time for you to spread the word and fight for Him. Who doesn't want to fight for their Father and everything that a Father is to do is done. You don't have to worry about food, shelter, enemies, etc. Anyone that loves their earthly father knows what I am speaking of. You are not going to let anyone say or do anything to hurt your father. We need to get that same appeal with God. He is the ultimate Father. When I don't understand something I ask Him and He gives me the direction. If I fall He is there waiting with His arms for me to make it back to Him. He isn't judging me yet! He is watching me and making sure that everything that is not of Him is not hurting me because I am doing His Will and walking towards the victory. I am worshipping Him in spirit and in truth. It is for certain that you have to want to serve Him there are going to be some avalanches waiting to see if you are going to let them bury you or if you are going to continue the journey. I know that the eyes of the Lord are on the righteous and His ears are open to their prayers. We are not justified by the works of the law but by faith in Jesus Christ. When we understand who we are then we come to the understanding as in Proverbs 20:24 Man's goings are of the LORD; how can a man then understand his own way? I am staying in a hotel room writing this book I have been taught from going through how to depend on God and everything that He speaks He means. When the word speaks and tells you that you are not to worry about food, clothing, shelter, etc. I am here to tell you that you don't have to worry about anything. This is found in

Luke 12: 29-34 29And seek not ye what ye shall eat, or what ye shall drink, neither be ye of doubtful mind. 30For all these things do the nations of the world seek after: and your Father knoweth that ye have need of these things. 31But rather seek ye the kingdom of God; and all these things shall be added unto you. 32Fear not, little flock; for it is your Father's good pleasure to give you the kingdom. 33Sell that ye have, and give alms; provide yourselves bags which wax not old, a treasure in the heavens that faileth not, where no thief approacheth, neither moth corrupteth. 34For where your treasure is, there will your heart be also. When God speaks listen to Him. Whatever He is trying to have be done for His Glory do it. Proverbs 3:7Be not wise in thine own eyes: fear the LORD, and depart from evil. God is not a respector of persons. He doesn't care who you are or your occupation if you fear God and work His righteousness you are accepted by Him. The gift of the Holy Spirit was poured out even on the Gentiles. Speaking in tongues and magnifying God. This is signifying that there is no difference in the Jews and the Gentiles. Please stop upsetting God. We have already lost the ability to live past one hundred and twenty years. Genesis 6:3. We are not doing what thus says the Lord as a whole world and God already sends us signs of this. God already has repented that He made us. We didn't make ourselves. God has already gone through the wickedness of man and that every imagination of our thoughts and our hearts we act out on the earth already. Can those that know better please start doing better and help those that are not able to help themselves. Love each other and fight for God not man. Make your Heavenly Father proud of you.

Father, On this road to wondrous opportunities being opened to me show me strength with Your arm and scatter the proud I am strong in the Lord and in the power of His might as in me Father let Your power work in me and then I will be amazed at Your power . I am in need of deliverance as I travel through this land I need the victory in this situation and only You can deliver me I call on the precious blood of Jesus I receive the benefits of the new covenant through the blood of Jesus. Surround me with songs of deliverance. Jesus resisted unto blood and gives me victory as the word states in Hebrews 12:4 The blood of Jesus bears witness to my deliverance and salvation Lord, keep my soul and deliver me. Be pleased, O Lord, to deliver me. Make haste, O God, and deliver me. Deliver me in Your righteousness. Deliver me from my prosecutors as I walk this journey for Your Glory. Help me and guide me through my footsteps as I walk this path that You have laid out for me. Deliver me from the oppression of man and take everything that is not of You out of me. I am delivered according to Your word.

Chapter 12

Power in Your Prayer

There is so much power in your prayer. None of us are perfect so don't let the naysayers tell you that He is not hearing what you are saying. They don't know what you are doing in your life to let the Light shine. You have to believe in what you are praying about. You cannot pray and then not truly take heed to what you said to God nor not believe that He is going to answer your prayer. I have heard "if they can speak to God and if they are doing this and that then they can raise the dead?" They may not be able to but I know that if you pray hard enough the ones that believe can raise that person up before he has gone to the grave. Case in point a man was in the hospital on his last leg his family called me and told me that he was not going to make it. I got down on my hands and knees and prayed as hard as I could that God just keep him until I got there to say good bye. But I told God if you keep him here (me being selfish or God using me to do His will you figure it out) a little longer then I will do everything that I can for Your kingdom. I will be the best of the best of them. That was my mission from that day forward. I wasn't a bad person I was walking into my destiny that is all. God was preparing me to speak to the masses and let them know what I have come to the knowledge of knowing. We don't place limitations on Him. That is the bottom line. I laugh when I hear any man tell me what they think God is not doing. God is not on a break He doesn't take a break on us we take a leave of absence on Him. Please don't believe the foolishness that we are not able to speak in tongue and speak to God essentially that is so far from the truth. After going to his death bed within the hour the man that was on his way out of this world was getting remedy for his situation. All I could do was thank God for what He was doing. I thanked God for letting me witness His Grace and Mercy not man but God….. But God…. That is such an awesome thing to watch a miracle manifest in your face. I am no longer on the street of "no He isn't" I don't go down the street of "that was then and this is now". The road that I travel is "Yes, He can." I know that not only can He I know that He does. This man was not eating, walking, barely talking, etc. He had given up and to even dig a little deeper it was so meant for it to be me. He has others around him that have healing hands. But God…. But God…. Chose little ole' me to make it there without me having a job and having any money. He sent me a miracle for me to go. He placed someone in my life to take great care of my kids as if it were me there. He was walking me through the whole process of trusting Him and letting Him get the glory. This is meaning something to someone. Every time I would walk in the room with him from that day to the day I left God was fixing him. This man started to eat and drink. He started coming back from the place where he was going. God was giving him a second chance and He was letting me see the awesome wonders that are spoken in His Word. Hello somebody. You have to get your own testimony to feel how great this feels if you are just sitting there and thinking that God didn't work a miracle. The devil is a liar. Within a few months this man gained all of his weight back and got back to life as he knew it. He is still shouting about his deliverance. God will make you do it. While there the enemy was fighting me but because I was listening to God He was telling me everything that was about to happen to me. He had to push some people away from me. I am not mad. I just know better so I do better. See the enemy was busy because he didn't want the manifestation to continue. I had to go through so I don't lean on my own understanding but on the understanding of Him that has placed me in a great place in my life. God is showing me and my children so many awesome things. I thought I could just get there I didn't realize that I had to go through to do it. I am not mad about anything that has happened to me nor am I mad at the people that He has placed out of my circle. I have learned to let go and let God. I don't have a circle I just have what I need and that is God, Jesus, and the Holy Spirit. I feel great with them around me and guiding me to the destiny that God has for me and my family. There are things that are going to happen to you to make you wish you would have never picked this book up not alone trying to get accurate with your gift. You are just getting prepared for your destiny. I know that I am going to be hated and torn by many but as I have come to learn man doesn't have a heaven or hell for me to go to. I don't want my Father saying to me "I told you to do it and you wouldn't do it." I

am doing it and with a smile I might add.
Everyone that had something new to man had to
go through something. This is not anything that is
new to man it is just something that has been laid
dormant in our church and it was so sad to know
what I knew and not be able to say "You are
wrong" because I was worried about what they
would say to me about me and my children. I
thought that my family meant everything to me
and that we meant everything to them. God had to
show me that it is all Him. I have been on this
path fighting for this to come out and learning
more about it myself. I don't know everything but
I know enough to stir up some fuss and get those
that are able to perform on their duties. Get on
top of your job people. As I was saying before I
lost my job and didn't have much of an income
coming in. God was showing me to trust Him. I
had to leave my home. I stayed with some relatives
and other relatives got so upset and indignant. I

would go to the bathroom and cry like a baby and tell my Father, "I don't know what to do I thought I was doing everything that you wanted me to do why are they so mean why are they lying on me and saying mean things to my children." I would cry out "Do you hear me?" I was lying in the bed in this person's house and just so depressed because I could see where God was taking me I just didn't want to go the way to get there. I was still depending on their love and support and now the love and support that was never really there was gone I knew that God was moving them out of my life. I have told my mother and my sister that when God shows out in my life they were not going to be there. I didn't know that my whole family was going to take the same seat as I had seen them take all of my life. The only thing that I know how to do is to pray. I would pray and pray until I fell asleep begging God to delivery me from this land. God keeps showing me a nice home. I was ready for it. All this was being shown to me to make me work that much harder to get it. I am working do you hear me. I have been placed in and out of a many lives from that day to this one to speak a Word into their lives. I know that you are around people for a reason. Find out what it is, deliver it, and get to the next phase. I went through so much I thought my heart was going to burst from the pain. Then God would minister to my spirit and tell me that it would be okay and that it is all in His time. I would awaken and pray for strength and courage to do His will and not mine. I would pray for the strength to let my family go as they had already let us go. We have been living in a hotel now for almost two years now. I am sitting here in awe writing this. I did just say that we have been living in a hotel for two years right? I did tell you that I haven't had a job given to me by man anyway? God is awesome. I know that I am getting out of this belly. My visions and dreams about this home are so vivid I can reach out and touch the banister. When you step out of what is considered normal the enemy is going to be on attack mode. True nothing that you are going to go through is going to be in vain it is all for your knowledge. If you didn't go through and God just told you to do this or that and then you will be at this point in your life you wouldn't do it would you? Well He did give you instruction to do many things and we as a collective have not been doing it until now. Break free and be different. Really follow His will and not theirs. They don't know what you know if they did I wouldn't have had to write this book now would I! When you go through with your family it makes you so much stronger to take on the world. Jesus is fighting this family with His family everyday as He takes on the world. Makes you think doesn't it. Through my prayer I received deliverance. Through my prayer I received a roof over my head and food on the table. I don't worry about anything. When He speaks to you and tells you that there is nothing to worry about because He is fighting this battle just give it to Him and believe that He is going to deliver you. He really does mean it. Those that don't understand the great and wonderful things that God is doing in our lives look and laugh at what is going on. My family is still saying horrid things behind my back. One of them tried to go and get my kids taken away from me he doesn't even know that I know about that. The information was not leaked to me by my earthly family. The information was delivered to me by my Father in heaven. I was a little hurt and disappointed more than anything but I just started praising His name and shouting and walking and shouting some more. He will deliver you from the hand of the enemy every time. You don't know all the time unless you have that type of relationship with Him. I Love that Man. I don't have to worry about anything at all. I cannot get a thought out of my mind about anything that I think is good and it is manifest in my face. I have been without money sometimes and go by a family members house to cook and clean to keep show them that I love them and what God is doing in my life and before I can get done they are giving me some money. I have travailed and told God I don't know how but I do know that You are going to do it. And when He does I cry boy do I cry. It feels good. I just know that you will feel His presence in the time of need. I had an individual that didn't even know me give me confirmation about this journey. It was getting hard. I would go to a prayer group every Tuesday (and still do) and couldn't make it back into their home without getting cursed out. My heart was so heavy with grief because these were my relatives. My relative went from not caring what everyone was telling her about us being in her home to she didn't know where we were going to be but we had to get out of her house. I fasted and prayed like you would not believe. I didn't have a job so there was no waiting for an income tax check. That is what some of the family members told her that my tax check should be coming and that I had to go. My relative let the rest of the family decide the date that we had to leave and God sent me some money and we have been in the hotel ever since waiting for our house. They would tell us after we prayed (which we do every day and night and in between time) that we needed to be quiet. We weren't loud at all. I wanted to melt sometimes and manifest when it was all over! I grew out of that. This is a growing process. I had to let go of the milk and my familiar and get into the unknown intimacy of God. There were many times that my children would get yelled at for something that someone else did. I can go on and on. All that had to happen so that I could get closer to God and let go and let Him. I was lying in the bed one afternoon. The kids were at school and she was fussing so it was a good day! I heard myself speaking in tongue I got up and said the devil is a liar. That is being told to you because that is how ignorant I was. This is the way that we are in our churches denying this for whom? I felt bad afterwards and I apologized and asked God to help me speak in tongue. I had to read my word and get the understanding as to what was happening to me. I couldn't ask anyone around me because none of them had spoken about this happening to them and they were Christians. I prayed and slowly but surely I have been speaking in tongue. I am telling you this so that when this occurs to you on your journey you don't deny the Holy Spirit don't be afraid of something different. Receive it in the name of Jesus. Let go and let God. One thing that you will learn is that the battle is truly not yours it is the Lords. The old me going through all of this would have given up already. The not having a home thing has happened to me before. I wasn't ready for what God was trying to do with me so I would give up and then find my own resolve and then eventually the same situation would happen again and then it would go away because I would again give up. This time like I was ready when I had gone to Texas I had already told God that I was not giving up before that. I had rededicated myself to fighting the good fight for real. The bottom line to this is the only family and friend you need to worry about they don't ask you for anything but for you to be right. They don't ask you for anything that they have given you back. You are not arguing with them nor are you fighting. God has given you the best combat tool in existence that is the power in your prayer. There are some of us that can pray. These are two great ones. Psalm 27 and 1 Chronicles 4:10

1The LORD is my light and my salvation; whom shall I fear? the LORD is the strength of my life; of whom shall I be afraid? 2When the wicked, even mine enemies and my foes, came upon me to eat up my flesh, they stumbled and fell. 3Though an host should encamp against me, my heart shall not fear: though war should rise against me, in this will I be confident. 4One thing have I desired of the LORD, that will I seek after; that I may dwell in the house of the LORD all the days of my life, to behold the beauty of the LORD, and to enquire in his temple. 5For in the time of trouble he shall hide me in his pavilion: in the secret of his tabernacle shall he hide me; he shall set me up upon a rock. 6And now shall mine head be lifted up above mine enemies round about me: therefore will I offer in his tabernacle sacrifices of joy; I will sing, yea, I will sing praises unto the LORD. 7Hear, O LORD, when I cry with my voice: have mercy also upon me, and answer me. 8When thou saidst, Seek ye my face; my heart said unto thee, Thy face, LORD, will I seek 9Hide not thy face far from me; put not thy servant away in anger: thou hast been my help; leave me not, neither forsake me, O God of my salvation. 10When my father and my mother forsake me, then the LORD will take me up 11Teach me thy way, O LORD, and lead me in a plain path, because of mine enemies. 12Deliver me not over unto the will of mine enemies: for false witnesses are risen up against me, and such as breathe out cruelty. 13I had fainted, unless I had believed to see the goodness of the LORD in the land of the living. 14Wait on the LORD: be of good courage, and he shall strengthen thine heart: wait, I say, on the LORD.

1 Chronicles 4: 10Oh that thou wouldest bless me indeed, and enlarge my coast, and that thine hand might be with me, and that thou wouldest keep me from evil, that it may not grieve me! And God granted him that which he requested.

Chapter 13

Praise

When was the last time that you praised Him for everything that He means to you? Take a moment out of your daily life and praise God. Take a moment and thank Jesus and praise Him for dying and resurrecting so you can have a chance at everlasting life. Lift your voice and exalt His praise You are Holy. He is wonderful and worthy of our praise. Shout unto God and give Him glory. God is merciful and mighty. When the praises go up blessings come down. When there are praises going up for a healing if it is the Will of God the healing will come down. When the praises go up power comes down. Praise Him. With long life He will satisfy you. One way this is done by being obedient to our parents. This is the first commandment given with a promise. God is not man that He should lie. Ephesians 6:2-3 2Honour thy father and mother; which is the first commandment with promise; 3That it may be well with thee, and thou mayest live long on the earth. Call on the name of the Lord He is worthy to be praised. 2 Samuel 22: 4I will call on the LORD, who is worthy to be praised: so shall I be saved from mine enemies. Praise His name and be delivered from those that call you everything but child of God. Deliverance comes out of your praise.1 Chronicles 16:35 And say ye, Save us, O God of our salvation, and gather us together, and deliver us from the heathen, that we may give thanks to thy holy name, and glory in thy praise. 2 Samuel 22: 50Therefore I will give thanks unto thee, O LORD, among the heathen, and I will sing praises unto thy name. Give thanks to Him with praises in song. God is to be feared and praised. 1 Chronicles 16: 25For great is the LORD, and greatly to be praised: he also is to be feared above all gods. We are human and many of us want to know how do we know that Alleluia is the highest praise. We only know that it is the praise that is used in heaven on many occasions throughout the word and when our heavenly brothers were able to see heaven they write that they saw or heard the angels giving praises and the word that was being spoken was "Alleluia" if it is worthy for them to say why not you? Say it and sing it and see how much deliverance is in speaking the highest praise that we are afforded to see in the Word. Revelation 19:1 And after these things I heard a great voice of much people in heaven, saying, Alleluia; Salvation, and glory, and honour, and power, unto the Lord our God: Revelation 19:3 And again they said, Alleluia And her smoke rose up for ever and ever. Revelation 19:4 And the four and twenty elders and the four beasts fell down and worshipped God that sat on the throne, saying, Amen; Alleluia. Revelation 19:6 And I heard as it were the voice of a great multitude, and as the voice of many waters, and as the voice of mighty thunderings, saying, Alleluia: for the Lord God omnipotent reigneth. Revelation 19:5And a voice came out of the throne, saying, Praise our God, all ye his servants, and ye that fear him, both small and great. You don't have to want a movement at all just telling Him thank You for all that You mean in my life. Thank You for waking me up this morning in my right mind. Thank You that I have some shelter from the weather and food in my home. Thank You that no one came into my home while I was asleep You protected me. Thank You for keeping Your angels around and about me and my family and keeping us from all hurt or danger. Thank You for answering the prayers of the righteous. Thank You for who You are and what You represent in my life. Take moments out of your day all day and give Him the praises that are due Him for being marvelous to you. It doesn't cost you anything and it means a multitude that is showing that you know who He is. Who else gets that Alleluia praise? No one that I know only God because He is awesome He is the Word. John 1: 1In the beginning was the Word, and the Word was with God, and the Word was God. 2The same was in the beginning with God. 3All things were made by him; and without him was not any thing made that was made. 4In him was life; and the life was the light of men. Let His light bring the darkness from you and shine you with His light so you are delivered from the darkness of this world and are able to make decisions that are worthy of you in His presence. Stop worrying about what is going on around you and worry about the one that can destroy both your body and your soul. These men on this earth don't have that power stop giving it to them stop being fearful because as I have stated and shown you in the word fear is not of God. Matthew 10:28And fear not them which kill the body, but are not able to kill the **soul**: but rather fear him which is able to destroy both soul and body in hell. There is no fear of man but of God. Isaiah 11:2 And the spirit of the LORD shall rest upon him, the spirit of wisdom and understanding, the spirit of counsel and might, the spirit of knowledge and of the fear of the LORD; 2 Timothy 1:7For God hath not given us the spirit of fear; but of power, and of love, and of a sound mind.

Father, I want to praise You with all my heart, mind, body, and soul. I thank you and praise you in the morning and all throughout the day. I bless Your name for who You are and what You mean in my life and to those that truly worship You in Spirit and in Truth. I praise You because You took time out of Your schedule and made me. You took the time to make this earth and everything in it. You took the time for us and I will always take the time to tell You Thank You and I Love You with my praises. You are a mighty God and I am serving You to the best of my ability teach me to be better. Let Your ways be my ways and help me to understand everything that is going on around me. Teach me to praise You in during the good times and the bad times as they are there to teach me. Let me learn the lessons that I need to learn so that I am a vessel to use to bring the lost sheep back into Your darling Son Jesus. Help me to see the flock as they are the wolf that has placed on sheep clothing. Teach me how to get myself together so that when I step into any location the enemy flees from the area. Teach me how to love my neighbor when he doesn't love me. Guide those around me that I am able to assist and those that are there to assist me with the good fight of faith. I love You and I will show You in my actions. In the name of Jesus I pray. Amen.

Chapter 14

He Wins!

No matter whose side you decide to be on. No matter if you decide to use your spiritual gifts. No matter if you let your friends and family guide you in what they feel is right. No matter what you do or how you do it in the end HE WINS. I don't know about you I just know that I came to realization that I am not here to serve man, woman, or child I am here to serve my God and help those that need the help to get to a place in God so they can help tend to the lost sheep. All of us are not going to except what is being fed to us only some of us. I am proud of myself that I have gotten to the place in my life where what anybody else has to say it doesn't mean anything to me. I know that I am on the winning team and that feels so awesome. I know that my coach is getting all of His best players in their proper areas and He is leading us to the greatest victory of all and it has already been written. He is so awesome He wrote the Word He is the Word and His Word is true and He doesn't lie because He isn't a man. His Word tells me that He cast everything that is evil into the pit of hell and it is abolished. How cool is that. You need to decide now whose team you are going to be on. I am in so much awe because it is written that He wins. I just think that is so cool. Everything that He has written will and has come and gone. He is so awesome He told you that He was going to win and you are still trying to make everyone around you happy and satisfied and they are making you miserable or they may be even placing a smile on your face for a small portion of time. Get out of the satisfying everyone and not God syndrome. That is a syndrome it is called sin.

Jesus ... Time to Stop Talking

It is my hope that something touched you to help you in your ministry for God's glory and grace. You have been Unty'd with Ty. To continue your Unty'd journey purchase books by yours truly at untydwithty.com. As you go through your trial and tribulation today remember to hold on and have hope and believe that God will be faithful that your deliverance is in your obedience.

Hold on Believe it and you shall receive it. Trouble doesn't last always. Storms prepare you for sunshine. If you would like to sponsor our efforts at Unty'd please do so at untydwithty.com and finally if you are not save, and wish to you must.

Hear the Gospel:

What is the Gospel? The death, burial, and resurrection of Christ Jesus 1 Corinthians 15:1-4 Moreover, brethren, I declare unto you the gospel which I preached unto you, which also ye have received, and wherein ye stand; By which also ye are saved, if ye keep in memory what I preached unto you, unless ye have believed in vain, For I delivered unto you first of all that which I also received, how that Christ died for our sins according to the scriptures: And that he was buried, and that he rose again the third day according to the scriptures:

How , then, can they call on the one they have not believed in? And how can they hear without someone preaching to them? Consequently, faith comes from hearing the message, and the message is heard through the work of Christ. Romans 10:14,17

Believe the Gospel:

Whoever believes and is baptized shall be saved, but whoever does not believe shall be damned. Mark 16:16

Repent:

Peter replied, "Repent and be baptized, every one of you, in the name of Jesus Christ so that your sins may be forgiven. And you will receive the gift of the Holy Spiritl Acts 2:38

Confess:

Whoever acknowledges me before men, I will also acknowledge him before my Father in Heaven. But whoever disowns me before men, I will disown him before my Father in Heaven. Matthew 10: 32-33

Be Baptized:

Peter replied, "Repent and be baptized, every one of you, in the name of Jesus Christ so that your sins may be forgiven. And you will receive the gift of the Holy Spirit. Acts 2:38

Remain Faithful Until Death:

While baptism puts us into Christ and washes away our sins, we must still be obedient and faithful to God, otherwise, we will lose our souls. The Bible tells us of the reward awaiting those who are faithful-

"...be thou faithful unto death, and I will give thee a crown of life." Revelation 2:10

Remember we are blessed to be a blessing.

Personal Invitation:

Deliverance by Faith, 4500 West Burleigh, Milwaukee WI. Not in Wisconsin you're invited to attend your nearest congregation.

Midwest Church of Christ, 609 West Center Street Milwaukee, WI

Other books by Tynesha Evans:

If you show him that you are honest, loyal, and trustworthy, and sexually responsible, then you will have the most powerful weapon to attract men. If you abuse your sexual power with many men it backfires on you. Most women realize this after they've had their " fun" when it's too late. Get your sense of value back for your sexuality. Sex may be fun and pleasurable don't forgot that it's the one gift that they can offer your husband, and that so many men place your value. Men place value on how pure we are.

BENEVOLENCE
REPLENISHED

We replenish our bank accounts, bellies, most of us our children, but what about those who have given you spiritually. The individuals who sow into our needs through prayer and supplication need to be replenished. There are some who may not even replenish themselves spiritually. This book allows you to P.U.S.H for yourself and others. There are scriptures that we need to speak to the mountains and make them remove themselves from our lives. Pray Until Something Happens!

TYNESHA EVANS
DON'T LET HIM
Practice on You

Since the beginning of our creation the Father placed matrimony in our lives. It is said that man cannot live alone. A man is to leave his mother and father and cleave become one with his wife. In today's society we have been so brain washed and made to believe that living in sin is okay. Most times Mr. Right now searches for the women that already has children. The women with children are the main focus of Mr. Right Now. Where does it say that this person has to move in with you? There are so many women placing the feelings of these men before their children's. The stats on kids running away are high. Prayer brings about change.

Tynesha Evans

Spiritual Gifts and the Church

There are so many of us that have been suppressing awesome gifts from God and it is time to stop so that our Churches grow as God wants them to. Did you know that knowledge is a spiritual gift? How about love? This book will enlighten you and strengthen you in your spiritual journey!

We all have our moments when we are tricked by disaster. The disaster may not be intentional. We may walk into a disaster that is truly not our own. How we respond to the disaster is evident to our destination in life. Our response is a key factor to the victory we are waiting for or the hell we go through before we let go and let God. He is speaking to us. He answers our requests. When we ask if the person is right for us He sends the answer are you listening to the response. (Fictional-Two Sister Spirit and Flesh Series)

THE FAMILIES OF TWO SISTERS
FRUIT OF THE SPIRIT AND WORKS OF THE FLESH SHORT STORY INTRODUCTIONS

BY TYNESHA EVANS

We all have family members that we tend to stay away from we may say a few prayers and wish them well. There are those around us that time and time again God has pushed out of our lives and our flesh pulls them back in the circle. Though we can't choose our families we can choose how we allow them to influence our lives. Through this series you will see everything that looks good is not always good for you. This series is designed to be an eye opener to build up the lost and to mend. It allows us to really evaluate the Works of the Flesh and the Fruit of the Spirit. Revealing the butt naked truth about how we allow the devil ammunition. We allow him to come in and keep us from the paths of righteousness we are predestined to walk with distraction after distraction. Read this series as we take back what the devil has stolen from you. Claim it and receive it in Jesus name. Amen (Fictional-Two Sister Spirit and Flesh Series)

Two Sisters
Spirit and Flesh

By Tynesha Evans

There are times when we must decide if we are going to live by the spirit or by the flesh. To make the journey to Heaven we have to be led by the spirit. We all fall down the victory is getting back up. Someone is watching you as you choose. Don't allow yourself to be blind sided by your trials and tribulations. The choices we make today will either hinder or bless someone to follow Christ. The word tells us if we make one stumble it would be better that a millstone be cast around our neck and we be cast into the deepest sea. Choose to make the right choice today. The things that you don't know can and do hurt. As you make strides to change your life strengthen your brother. Please enjoy the introduction of "Two Sisters Works of the Flesh and Fruits of the Spirit" a series of books as we continue to live our lives Christlike. Empowering Families Tyandkids.com (Fictional-Two Sister Spirit and Flesh Series)

This book is for the family member that I AM has said "Since you have asked for a discerning heart and not for long life or wealth for yourself, nor have asked for the death of your enemies but for discernment in administering justice, I will do what you have asked. I will give you a wise and discerning heart, so that there will never have been anyone like you, nor will there ever be. Moreover, I will give you what you have not asked for both riches and honor so that in your lifetime you will have no equal among kings. And if you walk in my ways and obey my statues and commands as David your father did, I will give you a long life" 1 Kings 3:10-14. It is time for you to awake and see that it is not a dream and with the powerful words in this book you are going to get to your destiny if it is God's Will. We are going to explore how not to react that family member(s) that get an enjoyment out of seeing you suffer. The solutions that are revealed in this book are tested and tried.

BASTARD MOLESTED BY CHESTER

BY CHESTER

FICTIONAL SERIES
BY TYNESHA EVANS

Chester only wanted to have his way with Bastard. He wanted to be taken care of. If only Bastard's mother would believe him. If only she didn't allow him to move in. If only she loved him more than this man! Please visit Tyandkids.com to purchase. (Fictional-Two Sister Spirit and Flesh Series)

Do you find yourself saying "I don't want to forgive them!" or perhaps someone else is having a difficult time letting go and giving it to God to move to a place of forgiveness. This book is the perfect gift for anyone having difficulty with forgiveness.

Lets Talk About Love!

By Tynesha Evans

WHAT THE LORD TELLS US ABOUT LOVE. WHO IS LOVE? THIS BOOK
GOES INTO THE DEPTHS OF WHAT LOVE IS.THIS IS JUST A PORTION
OF WHAT IS IN MY SPIRIT. THIS BOOK IS AN INSPIRATION AND I
KNOW THAT IT WILL HELP ALL OF US INCLUDING ME DEAL WITH
AGAPE! ENJOY.

I HAVE LEARNED WHATEVER STATE I'M IN TO BE CONTENT

Tynesha Evans

IF YOU ARE TIRED OF WONDERING WHY YOU ARE STILL GOING THROUGH WITHOUT ANY RESOLVE THIS BOOK IS FOR YOU. THERE MAY BE SOMETHING MISSING. CONTENTMENT. THERE MAY BE A SLIGHT CHANCE THAT YOU ARE OKAY WITH WHERE YOU ARE IN LIFE, BUT YOU ARE NOT CONTENT YOU ARE JUST EXISTING IN YOUR CIRCUMSTANCE. YOU ARE FAKING IT TO MAKE IT.

Untydwithty.com

9 781479 325764